Praise for *Student Equals Human*

In an educational atmosphere where pedagogy frequently contains more acronyms than actual substance, Adams reminds us of the fundamental humanity that should be the motivating force in our classrooms. With humor, clarity, and grace, his insights encourage us to reevaluate our roles as teachers, exhorting us to banish the hierarchical tendencies of our classes in favor of autonomy, curiosity, and respect. *Student Equals Human* is a call to compassion, a call that has never been more vital to educators.

—**Jessica Palmer**, educator and author of *The Ordering of Days*

Excellent, gently stinging points throughout . . . There is hope in these words for those who want to be better.

—**Jessica Shields**, counselor

I was a fantastic student in a traditional classroom setting. Unfortunately, this behavior made me feel like a doormat in a professional environment. "Unlearning" was a hard lesson to learn. I believe the ideas presented in *Student Equals Human* will empower students from the get-go to think critically, operate autonomously, and learn more efficiently. Teachers who embrace ideas about being more human will undoubtedly foster a classroom environment that builds better humans.

—**Maree Jones**, former student, social media strategist

Coach Adams believes in real freedom, the kind that comes with more responsibilities than perks. It was the greatest lesson: always treat the other as a human being.

—**Valeria Donado Levy**, former student, project manager

STUDENT EQUALS HUMAN

**THE SIMPLE EQUATION THAT
SAVED MY CLASSROOM (AND CAREER)**

JAY ADAMS

Student Equals Human: The Simple Equation That Saved My Classroom (and Career)
© 2020 Jay Adams

This book is available at special discounts when purchased in quantity for educational purposes or as premiums, promotions, or fundraisers. For inquiries and details, contact the publisher at books@daveburgessconsulting.com.

Published by Dave Burgess Consulting, Inc.
San Diego, CA
DaveBurgessConsulting.com

Library of Congress Control Number: 2020940829
Paperback ISBN: 978-1-951600-34-1
Ebook ISBN: 978-1-951600-35-8

Cover design by GOODSOUL
Interior design by Liz Schreiter
Editing and production by Reading List Editorial: readinglisteditorial.com

For Irma Jean. Thanks for ten thousand
issues of *Reader's Digest*.

For Laura. I'm glad we had Algebra II together.

And for every student. Thanks for being here;
you didn't have to be.

CONTENTS

INTRODUCTION

It's seven in the morning. Fifty million shoes are about to take a trip. Destination: sadness. Five days a week, thirty-six weeks out of every year, fifty million shoes deliver their owners to a building that makes them sad.

Those fifty million shoes are connected to twenty-five million students in grades 6 through 12. They'll board a bus, jump in a car, or take a walk. All those separate journeys will end in a very similar place: a classroom. And by 9 a.m., an alarming number of those human beings will feel like they're wasting their time—40 percent, in fact, who feel disengaged at school.[1] That's ten million bored human beings. Half of all middle school and high school students don't see a correlation between what they're learning at school and the real world.[2] Frustrated, disengaged, and bored out of their minds, twelve and a half million human beings spend most days wishing they were anywhere else on earth.

It's even worse than simple boredom and frustration: they'll also be unhappy 70 percent of the time and stressed out 80 percent of the time, according to a survey of twenty-two thousand students undertaken by Yale University and the Born This Way Foundation.[3] When

1   https://www.nap.edu/read/10421/chapter/1

2   http://www.youthtruthsurvey.org/student-engagement/

3   https://blogs.webmd.com/from-our-archives/20151026/students
    -unhappy-in-school-survey-finds

the survey asked students to describe their feelings about school, 75 percent of the words given in response were negative, with the three most common being *tired, stressed,* and *bored*. The takeaway from this distressing parade of numbers and adjectives is this: *school actively makes a lot of human beings sadder than they would otherwise be.* I am not okay with this.

Something is fundamentally broken in the school experience. No other industry would accept these kinds of customer satisfaction numbers. Walk into a Walmart and look around: their reasons will vary, but every single one of the shoppers made a conscious decision to shop there, and 75 percent of them say they're satisfied with the experience.[4] One hundred percent of the people at the movies on a Friday night want to be at the movies. One study even found that 95 percent of patients were satisfied with their colonoscopy experience.[5] Of course, school is neither Walmart nor a trip to the hospital. Still, I think it's not unreasonable to keep a baseline metric in mind: our students should be at least as happy as colonoscopy patients.

Given the sad state of affairs described above, there's one overwhelming fact that just doesn't fit: most teachers (including you!) are caring, highly motivated human beings who never set out to make their students sad. In fact, nearly 80 percent of teachers entered the profession specifically because they wanted to make a difference in the lives of young people.[6]

Consider the irony: precious few people work retail because they feel called to it as a means to change the world for the better, yet most customers in most retail establishments leave satisfied with the experience. Nearly every single person employed in a classroom chose

---

4 https://www.retaildive.com/news/survey-says-customers-more -pleased-with-wal-mart-stores/409015/

5 https://www.ncbi.nlm.nih.gov/pmc/articles/PMC2694655/

6 https://www.theguardian.com/teacher-network/2015/jan/27/five -top-reasons-teachers-join-and-quit

their career with the explicit goal of making a positive difference, yet most students leave frustrated each day. Something is clearly amiss.

How did we get here? What's broken? If human beings enter the world pre-wired to learn, and if schools are full of noble people like you, committed to helping them learn, where did things go wrong?

That's the question I found myself asking just a few years into my career. I spent three years as a teacher and coach, and it just wasn't working. I actually went part-time at the school so I could start doing pre-med classes at night, thinking that maybe I wanted to be a doctor instead. I spent two years wrapping up my classes, taking the MCAT, getting a good enough score for med school.

And then, sitting at my desk, with three completed med school applications in front of me, I realized: I'm a teacher. It's what I'm built to do. I could get into med school, sure. (Not Harvard, but somewhere.) I could become a doctor. But I couldn't picture myself actually doing much doctoring. The only medical job I could imagine enjoying was . . . teaching in a med school. And I couldn't see myself going into six-figure debt just to get back to doing what I was already doing.

I had almost talked myself into thinking that I wasn't supposed to be a teacher at all, when what I really needed was much simpler: I just needed to figure out how to be a *happy* teacher. I started reading relentlessly—every book about school and school culture I could get my hands on. I started tinkering with the way I managed my classes and interacted with students and parents.

And I realized that the issue might just have a fairly simple fix. The fundamental thing overlooked in many schools is a basic fact that's drilled into every retail worker's head: the customer's experience matters more than anything else. When schools have trouble grasping that they are in a customer service industry—and the customer is the student—things start to go off the rails in classrooms. When I figured out how to run my classroom in a way that explicitly considered my students—my customers—in very human terms, things started getting much simpler.

It's tempting to think that your customers are actually the parents or the taxpayers. It makes a certain amount of sense; after all, either the parents or the taxpayers are footing the bill. But I'm not sure the customer necessarily *has to be* the person paying the bill.

In a small town in Alabama, my friends Jamie and Amy Griffin run a children's party venue called Helena Hollow. Kids come to the Griffins' farm to pick pumpkins, pet the farm animals, and generally have a grand allergen-filled time. And here's the thing: Amy has never had a bunch of seven-year-olds whip out their Toddler Visa at closing time. Every single time, it's a mom or dad cutting the check. But guess who Amy focuses her efforts on, every single time?

Yup. The kids. Because she's figured out something that school systems seem programmed to forget: the customer isn't the person cutting the check; the customer is whoever holds veto power over the next transaction. Amy knows that if twelve kids get back in their parents' cars and say, "That was dumb and the lady was mean," then nobody's coming back to Helena Hollow for their next party, no matter how reasonable their prices are. Amy and Jamie recognize that veto power is the most important dynamic of their relationship with their customers; because they cannot pass laws forcing people to visit their llamas and emus and miniature cows, they better figure out how to build an environment that people will intentionally choose to experience.

My situation as a teacher isn't perfectly analogous to a petting zoo, of course. State law mandates that students attend school; as far as I know, students are not legally required to interact with llamas. In other words: people show up at Helena Hollow because they *want* to; people show up in class because they *have* to. But there are still lessons that transfer readily from one domain to the other.

Just like toddlers have veto power at the petting zoo, students have veto power in the classroom. This is because learning is the central transaction of the classroom—it's the only reason we're in the room—and students will always have the power to veto the learning experience. They hold all the cards. We can mandate their presence by law and use the court system to ensure compliance, yet the harsh truth remains: it is fundamentally impossible to force someone to learn against their will.[7]

Even if it were possible, it would be inefficient. I took piano lessons for years as a child, and I am a legitimately terrible piano player, because I didn't want to know how to play the piano—my mom wanted me to. On the other hand, I taught myself to play the guitar in just under six months when I was thirty, simply because I decided to do so on my own. This is the power of autonomy. (In fact, as I wrote that last line, my son ran into the room to tell me that he had spent the afternoon learning to spin a playing card so that it would fly back to him like a boomerang. I can think of no better illustration of the point I'm making than the joy on his face as he demonstrated this absolutely useless, yet freely chosen skill to me.)

Every day when they walk into my room, my students make a choice—either to engage, or to mentally check out. When I ask them to write, they can choose to think on paper deeply and incisively, or they can choose to jot down the first five hundred words that pop into their heads.[8] Teaching is hard enough; teaching unhappy people is impossible. But here's the secret: *We don't have to teach unhappy*

---

7 It occurred to me after writing this paragraph that you actually *can* force someone to learn against their will with the right incentive structure. It's just not ideal. Puppies learn pretty quickly with shock collars, and prisoners learn how to operate inside the prison system, simply to survive in a brutal environment. But I think neither shock collars nor prison rules are appropriate methods of classroom management, and I have to assume that you agree.

8 For the record, minimum word counts on essays are a bad idea, but that is outside the scope of this book. For a more thorough discussion, check out *Why They Can't Write* by John Warner.

people. We can teach people who actually don't mind being in our classrooms and (dare I say it) even look forward to the experience.

Simply put, our students are our customers, and happy customers are really easy to work with.

In fact, it's amazing how much *teacher* satisfaction is tied directly to the *student* experience. It turns out that if you crack the human code, you can start running a classroom that people don't hate being in, and most of the "classroom management" work takes care of itself. I've raised my voice in class three times in five years. It's been nearly a decade since I've filled out a disciplinary referral. And it's not because I simply let students be disrespectful or disruptive. In fact, I accomplish exactly what I set out to do most days. I lose far more class time to last-minute prom committee meetings than I do to disruptive students. It's also not because I put on a magical dog and pony show every day—or because I run a classroom chock-full of neat digital gizmos. That works for some teachers. But I have to teach in the personality I was given, and I am at heart a lecturer and discussion facilitator.

I am not a terribly creative person. I am not the smartest person in most rooms, and I am frequently outwitted by the technological tools I try to use to make my teaching life easier. What I am is a human being, keenly aware of my own humanity. And every day I walk into that classroom, I walk in with two very explicit, very concrete goals:

1. Model to my students what it means to be good at being a human being, and
2. Honor and value their humanity in a way that is intentional, obvious, and natural.

That's it. Those two goals are enough for me. Because, in a country facing a crisis of simple civility, learning to share humanity with other people is more valuable than any physics lesson or *Macbeth* lecture could ever be.

I'm in a unique position to think about these things: I'm a teacher *and* an administrator. In the interview process that landed me my current job as head of school, I insisted that I be able to keep teaching some courses. I think it's important that principals, headmasters, and other administrators keep one foot in the classroom. When we step completely out of the classroom, we begin to lose sight of the way our decisions affect the students and teachers for whom we are ultimately responsible. I like setting the course of an entire campus, but I am, at heart, a classroom teacher—which is why I feel so strongly about empowering other classroom teachers to run a more human classroom.

IN A COUNTRY FACING A CRISIS OF SIMPLE CIVILITY, LEARNING TO SHARE HUMANITY WITH OTHER PEOPLE IS MORE VALUABLE THAN ANY PHYSICS LESSON OR MACBETH LECTURE COULD EVER BE.

I'm primarily writing this book for three groups of people. Group One, the Wide-Eyed Optimists, consists of fairly new teachers or those about to become teachers. You got into this job to be Mr. Keating from *Dead Poets Society*, and I want to help make sure that you never lose that idealism. If you're in this group, you probably intuitively connect with many of the ideas you'll read here. I want to help crystallize some of your idealism into a coherent set of ideas about how teaching works.

I also want to make sure you understand: There are plenty of us out here who still approach each day of class with joy. You can be a Wide-Eyed Optimist as long as you want in this profession. If that's your goal, I want to tell you how I navigate the student-teacher relationship. I want to give you some vocabulary to talk about the phenomena that are common to all classrooms—because all classrooms are full of human beings. Most importantly, I want you to be a joyous little piece of friction in the system, breaking down the gears that grind students and teachers down and make them dread showing up each day.

Group Two is the Seasoned and Struggling; you may be more experienced educators, but your classrooms aren't working quite right anymore, your joy at coming to work is starting to wane, and you're starting to wonder if there's a better way. It's not your fault: maybe you were explicitly trained to view students as the enemy by terrible administrators, or maybe you unconsciously absorbed that message from incompetent ones. Either way, something major has shifted since you began teaching, and you're not sure why you're frustrated so often. I want to help you recover the simple joy of interacting with your students as people first, instead of thinking of them as learning objectives or disciplinary cases.

Or maybe you've never even really thought about how things could be any different; you're simply replicating the treatment you received at the hands of *your* teachers decades ago, and it's not getting the results you want in the classroom. I want to show you the other side, where students and teachers regard each other as peers.[9]

What does that look like in practice? I spent about an hour yesterday trading memes on Twitter with my students, as we sought to find the best picture or GIF to explain a moment from *Macbeth*. I spent an hour on the phone last week talking politics with a former

---

9   Not peers in the sense of position within the school; obviously, there is a fundamental power imbalance between students and teachers— otherwise, it wouldn't make any sense for the teacher to be the one leading the class. Rather, I mean peers in the sense of co-humans. Although I know more physics than my students do (most of the time), that does not mean I matter more than them, or that I can act arbitrarily because of that power imbalance. More on this in the chapter titled "Humans Matter Equally."

foreign exchange student. I routinely get terrible puns via text and social media in the middle of the day, because everyone who's ever been in my class knows that my favorite jokes are puns sufficiently awful to cause physical pain. A few years ago, a couple of my students taught me to play the guitar. None of those things happen in an adversarial scenario—they only happen when the classroom is viewed as a relationship among peers.

Group Three is the Vision Setters: the administrators who have to hire and train faculty, along with the teachers who are, whether in title or in practice, the show runners of their school. I've been in your shoes and sat on your side of the desk. I spent my first ten years in the classroom before spending the next six as head of school. I eventually walked away from that position, partly because I had been focusing on budgets and board meetings for so long, I was losing sight of how much joy could be found in a simple classroom.

When I started writing notes for this book years ago, I was trying to write the "How to Treat Students" manual I often wanted to hand my own struggling teachers, because I wanted them to enjoy the same rapport with students that made my life so much fun. In the process of writing, I got so into it that I actually stepped back into school administration, and I'm once again running a school. But as I pointed out earlier, teachers don't really know how to *not* teach, so I'll still be teaching my physics and American literature courses, as I have for the past decade or two.

No matter which group you're in, I hope you'll keep going on this journey with me. Because no matter what kind of educator you are, there's one principle that can change your career: in most businesses, success is tied, inevitably and inextricably, to human relationships. Learn to be human—openly and unashamedly—in front of your students. And learn the joy that comes with the relationships you'll develop once they figure out that they get to be human beings, too.

HUMAN HOMEWORK

1. Consider spending a class with your students evaluating their feelings about the purpose of school. I use a simple graphic for this. I have students consider each axis, then place a single dot at one (X,Y) coordinate that strikes them as the right "balance point." We chart the results to get the class average, then talk about each of the four goals. It never fails to generate a worthwhile discussion, and it gives me a philosophical anchor to refer back to throughout the course of the year—which is why I'll typically do it between weeks 3 and 4, once I've gotten to know them a bit.

2. Take a guess at what percentage of your students would identify as saddened, disengaged, or bored by school. Then survey them to compare it to your assumptions. Spend time talking through the results with them—and if you're really brave, invite parents in to talk about the results as well.

3. Make a list of the ways your students attempt to "veto" an educational transaction in your classroom. Then craft a plan to deal with it. For example, I tell my juniors and seniors on the first day of school that I will probably never tell them to put their phones away, as long as they're not distracting me or their classmates. If they can pass physics while tinkering on their phone, more power to them. Then I follow that up by telling them that if they *do* spend class time on their phones, and their parents express a concern about grades, I'll let the parents know how much time they spend on their phone and

recommend that the parents don't allow them to bring it to school anymore. In two minutes, I identify a potential source of future conflict, establish my credibility as a reasonable person, and ensure that if the phone ever becomes an issue, it won't be because of me. I've done this for a decade now, and it has caused exactly one issue in my classroom in ten years. I'll take that track record.

4. Make a list of those in your sphere of influence who don't seem to derive much joy from their teaching career anymore. Write down what it was about them that made you put them on the list. Then think about times when your own classes have gone poorly, and ask yourself if there is any overlap between your behavior in those classes and the behavior of the joyless teachers you've identified. (And, for goodness sake, DO NOT accidentally leave this list lying around or open on a screen somewhere.)

5. If you're on social media and permitted to interact with students, make a homework assignment out of it: "Tonight, everyone has to share a GIF that explains how you feel about the net ionic equations we worked out today."

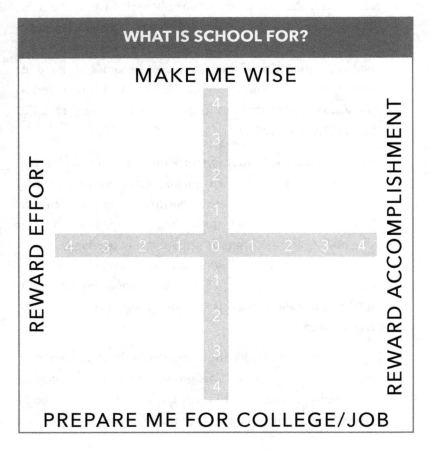

WHAT IS SCHOOL FOR?

MAKE ME WISE

REWARD EFFORT

REWARD ACCOMPLISHMENT

PREPARE ME FOR COLLEGE/JOB

(Note: Your students may be conditioned to read this graph as if up and right are positive and down and left are negative. Make sure you explain that there's no positive or negative value assigned to any quadrant, or they may give you the answer they think you want to hear rather than their honest opinion.)

ONE

HUMANS ARE ALIVE

*H*umans are alive. Or at least they're supposed to be. But look around. Some people wander the earth like the pre-dead: glassy-eyed, going through the motions, and generally morose. It's a modern malaise and a heartbreaking irony: in the most prosperous nation that's ever existed, with more material comfort than history has ever known, a lot of people are just marking time.

Tennyson summed it up famously in his poem "Ulysses," which makes me cry every year when we study it. Ulysses (whom you may know by the Greek name Odysseus) has returned to Ithaca from the Trojan War after decades wandering at sea. His son, Telemachus, has grown into a man in his absence. Ulysses's people no longer know him. But he is the king, returned from war, and he'd be well within his rights to resume the throne and while away his remaining days in power and luxury.

Instead, he gets back on a boat. Consumed with lust for adventure—for the moments when life crackled through his veins like electricity—Ulysses simply cannot go back to merely managing an island.

"How dull it is . . . To rust unburnished, not to shine in use! / As though to breathe were life." This is the line Tennyson puts in Ulysses's mouth right before he leaves his luxurious, secure Ithaca. Ulysses refuses to settle for a life that doesn't make him feel alive. How could he? After all, he is one of the "men that strove with gods." Ulysses understands what first-century theologian Irenaeus also grasped: "The glory of God is the living man," which often gets improved in mistranslation as "The glory of God is a man fully alive."[1] With that mindset, it's no wonder that managing the pre-modern version of the Ithaca DMV couldn't possibly matter that much to him.

Or could it? Ulysses's son, Telemachus, stays behind when his father heads back out to sea. I don't want to read too much into the text, but it seems Telemachus is perfectly happy in management. In the poem, Ulysses calls his son "blameless" and "decent," possessed of the "slow prudence" necessary to manage the mundane affairs of his father's kingdom. He closes simply, with "He works his work; I mine."

Embedded in this nineteenth-century poem is a fundamental idea: different things make different people feel alive, but everyone who's not pursuing life with vigor is wasting breath. Do we talk about this with our students? It's an important question: How do we teach students to pursue their passions when we occupy fifty-minute blocks of their time, against their will, all day long?

First, we need to slow down. Before we worry about why the kids don't want to be at school, let's ask a really difficult question: Why don't some of the adults?

The next few pages will be challenging, but I think they have to be. Anyone who's been in education for a reasonable amount of time has asked themselves: Why does it seem some teachers simply don't like students? Why are there *any* adults in our buildings who are perpetually frustrated, everlastingly cynical, dark harbingers of gloom?

---

1 https://en.wikiquote.org/wiki/Irenaeus

To be clear, I don't think it's likely that you're one of them. After all, you picked up this book, with its touchy-feely title and bright, inviting cover. But I bet you've asked these questions about some colleagues, at least inside your head. And they're legitimate questions. As we said earlier, the vast majority of teachers—nearly every single one of them—made a conscious choice to go into education specifically for the purpose of making a positive difference in the lives of their students. So what happened to the grumps? And why should you, an optimistic and idealistic soul, care?

On medieval maps, there were dragons. The point was to tell sailors where not to go. The point was to say, as clearly as possible: "Here there be dragons! Sail the other way!" And I think that's why we should spend some time thinking about the grumps—not because you're one of them, but because we want to make sure you sail the other way, especially if you're just starting out in your teaching journey.

Let's do a short math exercise. You won't need a calculator as long as you have five fingers and/or passed the first grade.

Very important question 1: How many workdays are there in a week?

Correct. There are generally five.

Very important question 2: How many days does a weekend contain?

Correct. Two. We generally think of Saturday and Sunday as the weekend. You're doing great so far.

Now for the crucial question: If the workweek is longer than the weekend, isn't it important that humans figure out how to love life during the week? From a purely mathematical perspective, if you have a choice between:

A. being happy for five days and sad on the weekend, or
B. being miserable for five days and happy on the weekend,

shouldn't you choose to be happy during the week, since it's going to be the larger chunk of your available life?

Of course, in an ideal world, you'd love every single day of your entire career. And certainly, there are people out there who absolutely love their lives all seven days of every week. Obviously, everyone aspires to be one of those people—and you may already be there, in which case you can skip this chapter.

As I stated earlier, I assume you're reading this because you've grown frustrated with your teaching life, or you're just starting out and you're worried about how to manage it, or because you want to help the teachers in your charge who seem to have lost their spark. In any case, I don't have a magic bullet to make anyone perfectly, perpetually happy. I just want to help people find the starting line on a track that leads to their own happiness.

The guiding principle of my career for the last decade and a half has been a single equation: Student = Human. That's what drives me to give my students the same sort of treatment that makes me happy with life. But here's the kicker: we can only do that if we're *actually* happy with life. It's not complicated. If we don't enjoy life during the week, we should focus on fixing that immediately, since the work-week consumes most of our conscious time on this planet. A shorter version: unhappy people can't be happy teachers, and unhappy teachers can't make happy students.

Remember those depressing statistics from the introduction about student opinions of school? Where do you think they learned those attitudes? From us. It shouldn't come as any surprise that 70 percent of students are unhappy at school if 67 percent of American adults feel disengaged from their jobs.[2] Amazingly, even though most people who go into education do so with a great sense of purpose and a keen desire to have a positive impact on the next generation, the statistics for workplace engagement are actually *worse* for

2   https://news.gallup.com/poll/188144/employee-engagement
    -stagnant-2015.aspx

teachers than the general public: 69 percent of teachers report feeling disengaged from their workplace.[3]

But let's not place the blame for a lack of workplace engagement squarely on the shoulders of the teachers. Instead, we should consider the possibility that teachers often feel disengaged for the very reasons their students do. In research that will shock precisely zero people who've actually spent time in a classroom, Richard Ingersoll of the University of Pennsylvania identifies a lack of autonomy due to bureaucratic micromanagement as the primary driver of teacher dissatisfaction.[4]

It's interesting to consider that the high rate of teacher burnout and massive dissatisfaction among students may stem from the same underlying cause: people like to be treated like human beings, and people assume that human beings should be free to set their own course. One crucial difference, of course, is that teachers are free to pursue another career—but every student has to keep showing up for school, one way or another.

If the primary stressor in your classroom is the result of a decision that's been made over your head, I empathize. Sadly, changing American education from the top down is going to take time, and it's going to require a critical mass of excellent teachers willing to clog up the gears of the machine. Figuring out how to make these kinds of waves is outside the scope of this book, and it's also not under your immediate control.

So let's focus on the things that *are* under your immediate control. Stop worrying for a minute about boosting test scores or funding a better lab or incorporating creativity into your lesson plans and just ask yourself: Are you the disengaged teacher? Nothing else matters much until you're honest with yourself about the answer. I

---

3   https://www.gallup.com/services/178709/state-america-schools
    -report.aspx

4   https://fee.org/articles/the-teacher-shortage-is-real-and-about-to
    -get-much-worse-heres-why/

always teach my students that a problem cannot be solved until we are willing to name it out loud. And I don't want to be harsh, but I do want to be honest. So let me say, delicately and up front: Nothing else I can write will help if you are a teacher who genuinely doesn't like being a teacher. If you don't like teaching, or don't like students, stop doing this job.

Right now.

I mean it. If you seriously don't like being a teacher, stop.[5]

. . .

. . .

I am *so glad* you're still here. I had a hunch that people who cared enough to buy this book would be willing to start by asking themselves the most fundamental question. Since you've gotten to this side of the question, we can assume a basic fact for the rest of the book: you love teaching, and you love the students you get to teach. Now it's just a matter of protecting and nurturing that love so that it's strong enough to pull you through an entire career.

It's important that we do this out loud in front of our students, because sometimes the rest of the world seems hell-bent on teaching them the opposite lesson. Every year as we approach graduation, I start seeing social media posts from adults who tell my seniors a lie with the best of intentions. They tell them, "Enjoy these last few months of high school! Soak it up, because it's all downhill from here. You're gonna wish you could go back one day."

---

5 Please don't think I mean you should jump out of the profession just because you had a rough semester or are going through a challenging season in your career. Struggling to carve out a classroom identity is something every teacher goes through at least a couple of times in their career. What I'm talking about here is something deeper: if you're genuinely unexcited about going to work, or find yourself counting down the minutes to the end of each day or each class, maybe it's time to consider a change. And maybe it doesn't even have to be a change of profession. Perhaps something as simple as adding a new course you care deeply about would work! In any event, the first step is always to name the problem, because only named problems can be solved.

STOP WORRYING FOR A MINUTE ABOUT BOOSTING TEST SCORES OR FUNDING A BETTER LAB OR INCORPORATING CREATIVITY INTO YOUR LESSON PLANS AND JUST ASK YOURSELF: ARE YOU THE DISENGAGED TEACHER?

It's a message that tends to hit my students hard, and every year I have to undo that damage. I tell them, "Never take advice from someone in middle age who hates their life so much they want to go back to high school.[6] Why would you take math advice from someone who stinks at math? Or let a terrible speller proofread your paper? Don't take life advice from people who dislike their own lives, just because they happen to be older than you."

I'd say that same thing to young teachers: If you love your job and you love your students, feel free to discount the advice and ignore the methods of any teachers around you who seem grumpy all the time. Find joyful teachers, watch what they do, and emulate whatever feels natural.

One of my favorite movies is *Say Anything*. There's a fantastic scene early in the movie where Lloyd Dobler (played by John Cusack) pretty effectively sums up my philosophy on this. He's being raised by his older sister, who's also serving as a single mom to her own rambunctious kickboxing toddler. At one point, the boy is kicking things around the apartment while his mom and big brother argue

---

6 Of course, some people saying this don't actually mean that they hate their lives; they simply mean that high school is a magical time before the realities and responsibilities of adult life set in. I trust that my students can tell the difference between an adult who is *nostalgic* for high school and an adult who *wishes they could return* to high school.

over something minor, and she just absolutely snaps at him. It's one of those terrifying mom-moments that freezes the room.

And Lloyd looks at his sister and calmly says, "Just be happy. I mean, how hard is it to just decide to be happy and . . . be happy?"

Listen to Lloyd. Just be happy, as a conscious decision, whenever possible.

Of course, I'm not suggesting that happiness is a switch that can be thrown on and off at will. Life is rarely as simple as a movie clip. Still, I think there's something to Lloyd's philosophy here, so I'll offer a slight edit: "How hard is it to just decide to move toward happiness? What if we adopted joy instead of stress as our default direction?"

In fact, Lloyd himself learns that happiness isn't a switch you can flip at will later in the movie, when he's dumped by Diane Court.[7] Rather than sulking passively,[8] he ignores the things he can't control and takes action on the things he can. In the movie's iconic scene, Lloyd drives to her house and stands in her driveway, boombox aloft, blasting Peter Gabriel's "In Your Eyes" through her bedroom window at roughly three hundred decibels.

I'm not suggesting that if you're going through a rough patch you should arrive at school tomorrow with a late-80s boombox blasting Peter Gabriel.[9] I'm simply pointing out that I want you to be happy, and if teaching doesn't make you feel joyously alive, you

---

7 She's played by Ione Skye. Look, I know I'm talking a lot about this movie, but I've been looking for a way to get paid to ramble at length about *Say Anything* for my entire career. Plus, this entire homage to the movie is an example of exactly what I'm talking about: it brings me joy to talk at length about one of my favorite movies, so I'm taking advantage of the opportunity. As I tell my students: take joy where you can find it; you don't know when the next opportunity will show up.

8 Which, okay, he does for a while, but give him a break—he gave her his heart, and she gave him a pen.

9 On the other hand, I'm also not *not* suggesting it. It's possible that such a move could make you a legend among your students, and there's never *really* a bad time to blast 80s movie soundtracks.

really only have three choices: consciously decide to change the way you approach the craft of teaching, stay frustrated, or get out of the business altogether.

And no one wants you to get out of the business altogether. Again, you bought a book about how to value your students as human beings. You think about these things. *You're one of the good ones.* But sometimes even the good ones find themselves perpetually frustrated.

And no one wins in a classroom staffed by a perpetually frustrated adult. Students don't learn, because students don't respond to grumpy teachers. Parents aren't satisfied, because no one likes to leave their child in the hands of a cynical, angry person. Administrators aren't happy, because unhappy teachers make for miserable students, parents, and bosses. And other teachers *really* aren't happy, because teachers who convince students that adult life is miserable make it SO VERY MUCH HARDER for the rest of us to convince them that, actually, life is pretty awesome.

So if quitting is not an option, and staying frustrated isn't an option, we've only got one path left: to work to reclaim the joy of teaching. You can't become joyful overnight. But if you're honest and willing to work (which you are, or you wouldn't still be reading), you can make an intentional decision to begin moving in the direction of happiness, and that shift will become obvious to your students very quickly.

I know talking about unhappiness and frustration can be uncomfortable; this section of the book has been through about eleven drafts by now. But teaching is about the pursuit and communication of truth, even when that truth makes us uncomfortable. My goals are simple: I want all of our students to have teachers who like being in the building with them every day. I want teachers in my school to love teaching—and love the students they teach—as much as the best teachers I know do.

It's really quite simple: *I want you to feel alive* the way Ulysses did. I want the world to know what you are like when you are happy. And I know that both you and your students are best served if you start that journey as quickly as possible, because joyful people who love their jobs out loud are positively intriguing to teenagers.

There's another sad poem that I teach every year. (I teach a lot of sad poems, which is odd because I'm a generally goofy person.) T. S. Eliot's poem "The Love Song of J. Alfred Prufrock" is voiced by a timid man who has been cowed by the world around him. Unlike Ulysses, he is too terrified of the possibility of failure to risk anything. He would never dream of getting back in the boat. He'd walk to the dock and dream about getting on the boat, but he'd never risk actually crossing the gangplank.

The poem's central journey consists of Prufrock walking to a party, fantasizing about all the wonderful things that will happen when he gets there. It's a world of fantastic possibility—but at the crucial moment, he turns and walks back down the host's steps. He never even rings the doorbell. Afraid of making the wrong impression, he chooses to make no impression at all.

At one point, conjuring up the perfect image to convey the static meaninglessness of his existence, Prufrock speaks: "I have measured out my life with coffee spoons." It's a simple, staggering picture: in the space of nine words, we see the past thirty years and the next thirty years of Prufrock's life, one routine scoop of coffee after another, morning by morning . . . forever.

I feel for the teachers who are in this boat, and I'm driven to help as many as I can. I think a lot of teachers count lesson plans the way Prufrock counted coffee spoons. I once knew a teacher who taught the same lessons, in the same order, on the same days—for years. On the first day of school, her entire year was already laid out in front of her, just like every year before. She did not seem alive to me. She seemed like the teacher version of a Roomba, mindlessly puttering through her job each day just to head to home base and recharge overnight before doing the exact same thing the next day. Coffee spoons.

It's impossible to inspire students to live giant, meaningful, audacious lives if they don't think you're doing the same thing. It's impossible to make students value their time with you if they sense that you're counting the hours until three o'clock on Friday. They listen to you about history because they trust that you know more history. They follow your directions in math because they trust that you know more math.

But do they believe you know more about being truly *alive*?

IT'S IMPOSSIBLE TO INSPIRE STUDENTS TO LIVE GIANT, MEANINGFUL, AUDACIOUS LIVES IF THEY DON'T THINK YOU'RE DOING THE SAME THING.

HUMAN HOMEWORK

Get to a place where you can think uninterrupted for a while, and answer these questions:

1. What are the last three things you remember consciously loving about your job? Describe them in detail: Where were you? Who was in the room? What specific tasks were you handling? How could you arrange your life to experience them more—even if it meant changing your employer or career?

2. What are the last three things you remember consciously hating about your job? Describe them in detail: Where were you? Who was in the room? What specific tasks were involved? How could you minimize those things so you experience them less?

3. Print out a ten-day calendar and draw a diagonal line to split each day into two parts. Each night, before you go to bed, rate your eagerness to go to work the next day, where 10 equals "I can't wait to get there" and 0 equals "I would literally rather eat a handful of glass." Each afternoon, before you leave school, rate how the day went, where 10 equals "I had an absolute blast today" and 0 equals "I'm picking up a Starbucks application on the way home." After two weeks, average your scores, look for patterns, and discuss them with a spouse, partner, or trusted friend.

4. Answer these questions: Do my students believe I like my job? How do I know? Do my students believe I know what I'm talking about? How do I know? Do my students believe I like them as human beings? How do I know? (One effective way to do this is to set up a simple anonymous Google

form with these questions and ask students to complete it. Though I am typically opposed to anonymous feedback, I think in this case it's vital—especially the first time you try it. If you do it a couple of times in a row, and the students see that their feedback has an impact on the classroom, you can add the "Name" field back to the form and they'll trust you enough to be honest with their name attached.)

5. If you do this exact thing every day for the next five years, will you consider those five years a success? Imagine your life in five years if you change nothing, then free write about it for five minutes. What would that look like? How would you feel? Read over what you've written. Is it mostly positive? Mostly negative? Neutral?

6. If you had a money faucet in your house so you didn't have to worry about bills, would you keep doing what you're doing with your life? If the answer to that question is no, what would you do instead?

After answering those questions, you should have a sense of where you are in terms of job satisfaction. Those are the questions I ask myself at the end of every year, when I'm deciding whether or not to stay in my current role. Most years, I find out I still love what I do. In my career, I've only landed at "It's time to do something different" three times, and in those cases I realized I didn't actually want to leave education, I just wanted to change the specific job I was doing in education.

I've gotten some criticism about question number six before. People say, "Well, obviously, no one would keep working if they had a money faucet in their house, even if they loved their job. That's ridiculous."

And that is actually the saddest thing about doing this exercise. Because the world abounds with examples of people who will never need to work again, yet they keep showing up at their job or they go find a new challenge. Steve Jobs did not keep refining the iPhone because he was worried about making the car payment. Does anyone harbor the illusion that Tom Brady keeps playing football to pad his 401(k)?

No. These are people who have accumulated so much wealth that their children's children will still be able to wallpaper their bathroom with hundred-dollar bills, and yet they just . . . keep . . . showing . . . up.

Why?

Because when a rational human finds the thing they love, they keep doing it until they can't do it anymore. And we owe it to our students to model this kind of person. Schools should be filled with people who are fully alive, because students deserve to be surrounded by adults who love what they do. To accept anything else would be cynical beyond comprehension.

So go do your homework, and decide if, right now, being a teacher is Ulysses's boat or Prufrock's coffee spoons for you. If you're in the world of coffee spoons, I want to help, and I'd love it if you'd head to my website and fill out a short form,[10] so we can talk about what you could do next. If the answer is Ulysses's boat, don't worry: now that the big stuff is out of the way, we're going to start talking about steps you can take to completely change the teacher-student experience in your classroom.

---

10 https://www.studentequalshuman.com/join-humans

HUMANS MATTER EQUALLY

I f you've read this far, you believe there's some value to what I'm telling you. Now let's talk about what is (I believe) the most fundamental shift in thinking that will be required of you. And it will likely be very uncomfortable, particularly for those who were raised in (or trained in) an environment that drew rigid distinctions between teacher and student.

First, answer this: What separates me from the students? What makes me the chemistry teacher? Was my position handed down from the heavens? Did I pull the Chemistry Sword from the stone, or get my teaching certificate from the Lady of the Lake?

That's really the most fundamental thing, right? If I can't explain what makes me the chemistry teacher, why should anyone listen to me about chemistry?

Let's start by listing some incorrect answers:

1. **I am older.** True, but that's not why I'm the chemistry teacher. The school resource officer is also older than the students. And they probably don't ask him for help balancing redox reactions.

2. **I have a degree or certificate.** True, but that's not why I'm the chemistry teacher. There are people everywhere with degrees and certificates, but only *I* have been tasked with teaching chemistry in *my* classroom.
3. **I'm getting paid to show up.** True, but that's not why I'm the chemistry teacher. The secretaries are getting paid to show up, but no one is asking them to teach chemistry.
4. **I was hired specifically to teach chemistry.** True, but that doesn't make me a chemistry teacher. You *could* hire me to perform neurosurgery, but I assure you that would not make me a neurosurgeon, and I dare say you shouldn't let me saw your skull open on that basis.

As it turns out, there are exactly two facts that make me the chemistry teacher in my classroom:

1. I actually know how to do the stuff in the chemistry book.
2. I have been asked to share that knowledge with people who want to learn it.

If those two sentences are true of you, then you are also a teacher. Here's an interesting corollary to this idea: whatever your subject, any student in your room who is sharing their knowledge with other students is *also* a teacher. And they're doing it for free, unlike you, a heartless mercenary who expects a paycheck for it.

I'm kidding, of course. I don't fault you for expecting a paycheck; I also expect a paycheck, since I value my abilities and expect others to value them similarly. What I am saying is that two things, and only two things, make you "the teacher": your body of knowledge and your willingness to share it. That's all warm and fuzzy and nice-feeling, right? It turns out you're not a mercenary, after all—you're a saint.

Maybe not. Because a whole host of unconscious habits and behaviors stems from those incorrect assumptions we started with.

In practice, many teachers (accidentally or on purpose) convey the message "*Because* I am the teacher, I am more important than you." These subtle little moments worm their way into classrooms, where they begin eating away at the relationship between teacher and student, creating disharmony and making everyone's life more difficult.

Maybe you don't believe you're sending that message. But ask yourself a few questions. Do you:

1. Expect students to be on time for your class without fail, but permit yourself to be late sometimes?
2. Expect students to stand in line at lunch, while you go to the special "teacher spot" where you get served first?
3. Expect students to hand in assignments on time, while you often turn in grades or lesson plans late? Or take forever to return assignments?
4. Expect students to keep their phones put away, but sometimes pull yours out for something other than school-related work?
5. Refuse to allow drinks or snacks in class, but teach with a coffee cup in your hand all day and a supply of snacks in your top desk drawer?
6. Punish students for "plagiarism," but scour the internet for worksheets you can use instead of writing your own?
7. Expect students to do four hundred pages of reading over the summer without making yourself do four hundred pages of professional development reading?
8. Get angry if students talk while you're teaching, but keep a running commentary going with your buddies during staff meetings and professional development?

(Let me pause here to say how grateful I am that you didn't throw anything at me while we went down this list.)

This list could have been a million lines long. After nearly twenty years in education, I have seen all manner of behavior by adults—self included—justified under the umbrella excuse of "I get to do this because I'm the *grownup!*" When I'm honest with myself, I constantly catch myself saddling students with expectations that I unconsciously give myself permission to neglect. This test of character—which I often fail—brings with it a moment of choice, every time: either I alter my behavior or my policies so that I'm operating with integrity, or I send the message to my students that "because I am a teacher, I am free to ignore the rules. This is the power of adulthood."

It's not just about what we do in school contexts, either: it's about the rest of life as well. Do we drive a bit over the speed limit, but lose it if a student pushes a boundary? Do we dislike students who seek the loopholes in school rules, but spend hours looking for tax loopholes each April? Do we complain about the students' work ethic, but also complain with other teachers when we're asked to do something extra?

And after surveying and polling and discussing and interacting with hundreds of students—and after a long, hard look at my own failures in this regard—I am here to tell you: This hierarchical thinking *is* the enemy. It's the largest thing standing between us and our students. A system in which rules are arbitrarily created and applied is tyranny, in which "right" depends on the position, mood, and the inscrutable internal logic of the ruler. A system in which rules are systematically, yet unfairly, applied is a caste system, in which some people enjoy a different set of rules "just because." My British literature students came up with a sentence during a *Lord of the Flies* discussion that works really well here: "A rule that's applied unevenly isn't a rule; it's a weapon."

Similarly, "I graduated from college" and "I worked to earn the right to be here" are not adequate justifications for hypocritical expectations of students. As a parent, I want to send my kids to teachers who are there to *serve* them each day, not to teachers who are there to *rule* them. And if you're uncomfortable thinking about education as a customer service job, just know that I once was too, but changing my mind made my life immeasurably better. I certainly hope you'll keep reading long enough to come around to my way of thinking about this.

The irony, of course, is that we inhabit a country founded on the principle that every individual is "created equal," but we run an educational system that often subverts the very messages we try to communicate in our history and civics courses. It amazes me that there so many adults call talk radio or post on social media to decry what they perceive as capricious and arbitrary tyranny by large-scale government, yet they unconsciously and unquestioningly accept it in the classrooms of their local schools. (Or, worse, they actually think this way *intentionally* and celebrate it, under the misguided assumption that arbitrary rule-badgering "makes kids look forward to being adults" or some such gibberish.)

Teaching is about relationships, and any relationship that routinely finds itself at "Because I said so" is a relationship in trouble. It only shifts the problem to the next generation, as another batch of students becomes a new batch of adults who think it is their right to exercise their irrational and arbitrary will against the weaker, the younger, and the smaller.

It does sound kind of bleak when I say it that way, doesn't it?

Here's a thing I've heard a lot of: "But Jay, students have to learn to follow rules. The adult world is full of rules, and it's important that they learn to deal with reality."

Yes. And no. Of course, there are rules. But also:

1. The average speed driven on American highways is 4–7 mph higher than posted limits. We have collectively decided that the speed limit doesn't really matter, even though we spend billions of tax dollars producing, maintaining, and enforcing speed limit signs. So our nit-picking over dress codes may seem irrational to students, who observe most adults casually ignoring clearly posted state law when it serves their purposes.

2. If you don't get your federal taxes done on time, you can ask the IRS for a few more weeks. Fifteen million people do, every single year.[1] And the IRS nearly always grants extensions with no penalty. So our insistence that Comprehension Check 3.4 must absolutely be done by Tuesday at 11:10 a.m. may seem a bit misplaced to many students.

3. There are plenty of businesses that allow employees to have drinks and snacks virtually any time they want. Your accountant is going to have a cup of coffee on his desk. The rental-car clerk will have a soft drink within arm's reach. So the "no food or drink" rule can't actually be about teaching students to deal with the "rules of the workplace."

In short, students are frustrated by schools. They're frustrated because many of them begin the day by pledging allegiance to the flag of a country where everyone is "endowed by their Creator with certain unalienable rights," yet they feel as if they are treated as subhuman merely because of their age and station.

Of course, rules and rights aren't exactly analogous, nor can they be; nevertheless, students love and respect teachers who make a good-faith effort to connect the two, who are open to explaining why they diverge if and when they do so, and who affirm the value and equality of all people in words *and* in practice. There are plenty of simple ways to start trying to do this; your mileage may vary:

1. Stand in the same lunch line as students. What if you have work to do that requires you to get your lunch early? You should politely ask, like a human: "I have a stack of papers to grade. Do you mind if I get my lunch ahead of you?" I promise they will say yes, almost without fail.

2. If you hand a graded assignment back a bit late, give each student a pass that lets them turn in one assignment late as

---

1   https://www.irs.gov/newsroom/some-people-get-more-time-to-file -without-asking-anyone-else-can-request-an-automatic-extension

well. Or, better, just run a classroom with as few hard dead-lines as possible and teach students how to negotiate reasonably when they hit an unavoidable snag.

3. If you get to class late, try telling them that you will start tomorrow's class five minutes late to "give them back the time I wasted." Or, better, don't be the kind of teacher who loses their mind over airtight schedules.

4. Don't make students ask for permission to pee.[2] You don't make your own children ask for permission to pee at home. What changes at school? Is the building magic? Average workers in America don't have to routinely ask for permission to go to the restroom. They are trusted to attend to their own biological needs in a way that causes minimal disturbance to their work. Want proof of how weird permission to pee is? Try this: send your principal a text during your free period asking him if he minds if you go pee. Observe his completely freaked-out response. The next time you're out to eat, ask the waiter: "Before you take our order, do you think the manager will mind if I go pee?" He will not think you are normal.

5. Don't make them raise their hand to talk every single time.[3] When you're in a faculty meeting, do you raise your hand to talk? Maybe you do; I never have. I wait for a natural break in the conversation and jump in politely. And we certainly don't do it around the dinner table when discussing something important with family and friends. Why run your

---

2 I am aware that some teachers will shake their head at this; I insist that, if we genuinely don't feel we can trust adolescents to manage a simple trip to the bathroom, we have a much larger societal problem than the bathroom.

3 I say "every single time" because there are obvious limitations to this philosophy that will vary widely from classroom to classroom and lesson to lesson.

classroom like it's a Fortune 500 shareholder meeting, where people have to line up for a turn at the microphone? Your classroom is a conversation, so teach your students how to converse with civility. Teach them how to wait their turn and read social cues. Teach them the difference between a formal meeting and a group chat. That makes sense to them and works far better than trying to condition them to do something they don't typically see adults subjected to.

So start tomorrow, by taking time to ask your class this question: "Why do you guys think I am the teacher? What makes me different from you?"

Be explicit in helping them understand these things:

- I don't matter more than you.
- At the moment, I happen to know more [history/algebra/etc.] than you do.
- I want to share what I know with you, and here's why. (Reasons may vary.)
- On most days, I want this classroom to feel like a conversation, not a formal meeting.

There are a thousand other ways you can put this principle into practice. For today, make a short list of three things you can do tomorrow to demonstrate to students that you are not more *important* than they are just because you know more algebra (or history or art or math). Your list may look different than mine,[4] since you know the culture of your school and students far better than I can.

What I do know is this: as you start looking for ways to see your students as peers, you'll find more, and the students-as-equals

---

4 My original list, years ago, was 1. thank them for coming to class; 2. stand in the lunch line with them; and 3. instead of telling them when the test will be, give them a few options and ask which day works best for the class.

lifestyle will soon become unconscious. I remember the first moment a student asked me: "Coach, why do you stand in line with us when they would give you your food behind the counter faster?"

AS YOU START LOOKING FOR WAYS TO SEE YOUR STUDENTS AS PEERS, YOU'LL FIND MORE, AND THE STUDENTS-AS-EQUALS LIFESTYLE WILL SOON BECOME UNCONSCIOUS.

My answer was simple: "If I needed to eat fast, I would ask to move up. But since I don't, there's no reason for me to cut the line. If I walked into McDonald's and just cut in front of all the teenagers, I would be a tremendous jerk. I assume that logic also applies at school."

She absorbed that, went back to her table, and told her friends what I said. They asked about it later in class, leading to a wide-ranging and engaging discussion about authority, the roles of teachers and students, and where both teachers and students typically get things wrong.

The discussion touched on the foundations of our educational system, the principles of ethical leadership, the natural-rights concepts undergirding the Constitution and Bill of Rights, political theory, and much more. It was *way* better than the chemistry lesson I had planned.

I've always been fortunate enough to trip into these sorts of off-the-cuff teachable moments; I suspect that may have something to do with the fact that I am hardwired to point out behavioral inconsistencies in authority figures. If you're not wired that way, you may have to spend more time and energy forcing the issue.

One way to do this is to simply set aside some time to discuss the reasoning behind the policies in your class with your students. You might do this by taking fifteen minutes each week to explain one rule and allow for a Q&A about it. Or you might devote a couple of class days up front to tackle it all at once. Either way, it's crucial that you communicate to your students two foundational principles about the rules in your room:

1. They are not arbitrary or capricious. To the contrary, they are deeply considered, vitally necessary, and you have taken great pains to write only as many rules as are required to run class smoothly.
2. You are willing to hold yourself accountable to the same standard you are imposing on them.

Be warned—this may upset some teachers.

"I'm not standing in line with the students," a teacher once told me. "I've worked too hard and too long, and believe I've at least earned the right to not wait for lunch."

That teacher gave away the opportunity to actively communicate a fundamental principle of human worth to students. Actually, the teacher in question didn't even give it away; they traded it, every day, for lunchroom chicken nuggets.

To that teacher, I would say: Sure. If you have negotiated in your contract the right to eat first, and the entity that hired you consented to make "speedy and efficient lunch" a condition of your employment, then you are absolutely technically correct. But if not, you are telling every student in the school (and every teacher that stands in line with them) that you matter just a little bit more than they do. And so, collectively, we discount your opinion. It simply doesn't matter, since you've chosen to value the exercise of power more than the application of reason.

Too harsh?

I don't think so.

You're an algebra teacher because you are teaching algebra. I'm a chemistry teacher because I am teaching chemistry. Beyond that, none of us are more special than our students are just because we're older, taller, wealthier, or more stressed out.

Everyone in your classroom has different talents, abilities, skills, struggles, and baggage. But everyone in your classroom matters equally. Because everyone in your classroom—including you—is a human being.

HUMAN HOMEWORK

1. Make two columns: "Meaningful ways I exercise my authority" and "Counterproductive ways I exercise my authority." Evaluate yourself. For example, in my "Meaningful" column, I recently had an entry that read, "I tweaked my attendance/tardy policy so that it more closely reflected what students could expect in a collegiate classroom, and took the time to explain why the change was necessary." In "Counterproductive," I almost always have something along the lines of "I made decision [X] without adequately considering all sides, and wound up having to walk it back after the fact." If you're honest, you'll have plenty in both columns. Each week, work on eliminating one item from the Counterproductive column and coming up with a new entry for the Meaningful column.

2. Ask students to make a list of class laws or rules that don't make sense to them. Use a Google form or Pear Deck to

collect answers, then discuss the most common entries. For the items that much of the class has noticed, ask them to consider the other side: Why might someone in authority want this rule to exist? You may be able to convince them that some are worthwhile; on the other hand, you may have to say, "I don't get it, either" on some of them. In any case, your willingness to simply discuss it and care about their opinion will matter immensely to them.

3. Go through every rule you commonly enforce, and ask yourself: Are there areas where my students see me being hypocritical in this area? If you're really brave, ask them to tell you what they've noticed.

4. Find one way to visibly communicate to students, without words, this message: "I am with you, and I don't matter more than you." As I've mentioned elsewhere, I try to start each class by genuinely thanking students for being in the room. I sit close to the student section at basketball games. I go into the elementary lunchroom a few times a week to collect fist bumps. This may seem manipulative, but if I notice trash on the hallway floor, I wait until the break between classes to pick it up, because I want them to know that I don't think of it as someone else's job. What works for you will vary, but do something intentional. Do it until someone notices. If no one notices after a month, it's not working, so try a different way.

THREE

BUT NOT ALL OUTCOMES ARE EQUAL. HUMANS CHOOSE.

I love words. I like to play with them in my head, roll them around in my mouth, learn where they came from and what they've meant over the years. Words can remake the world. They've done it over and over again throughout history. They're powerful. But words are dangerous when they're used loosely, and I think that's a special danger attached to the word *equality*.

Every year, our school gets a report from the ACT identifying how many of our students meet the "college readiness benchmarks" in the content areas tested by the ACT. It has some value as a metric, I suppose. But it tempts us with a pernicious lie: that all students should go to college. That's simply not true.

One reason it's not true is tied to marketplace practicality: if every student currently in America receives a college diploma, then a college diploma in 2050 will only be as valuable as a high school diploma is at the present moment. A bachelor's degree would lose all value as an indicator of educational attainment or academic ability. In fact, we're already beginning to see this phenomenon, as jobs that once were attainable with a high school diploma began to require a bachelor's degree, and jobs that required a bachelor's degree now require a master's degree.

Another reason is rooted in liberty: not all students desire or need a college degree to acquire the life they want to create. The relentless drive to create equal outcomes for all students assumes that they should all want the same thing, and it seems presumptuous to force them to prepare for a life they're not choosing. We may disagree about the point at which students should be free to select their own outcomes in life, but hopefully we can agree that expanding a system that currently requires twelve years of a student's life and extending it to tack on four more years of effectively mandatory schooling is a step backward.

The simple fact is that, as humans mature, they begin to desire influence over the outcome of their lives. Some will get there faster than others. Some will choose well, and some will choose poorly. Some will play it safe, some will throw caution to the wind, and some will choose not to try very hard.

In my classroom, I'm clear with my students about this. I made a poster in Canva that hangs on my wall. It has a picture of a rocket over the words *Launch Pad*, and the copy at the bottom says, "You can go wherever you choose from this classroom." Around the rocket, I've listed the jobs that my former students now have as adults, and I've intentionally listed jobs from all economic sectors: photographer, pharmacy tech, doctor, stay-at-home parent, construction company owner, nutritionist, teacher, dance instructor, and more.

I'm sending a couple of messages when we talk about this poster early in the year. One lesson is this: until you invest in your own life by taking control of its direction, it's likely that nothing we do in this classroom will matter to you very much.

The second lesson is this: I'm not going to judge your worth as a person based on what you choose. Some of my students are drawn to medicine. They're going to need to prepare themselves for college quite aggressively. Some of my students plan to take over their dad's landscaping business. British literature really won't be a requirement for that job. Fortunately, I teach math, science, and literature, so I can typically find a way to click with each student in at least one of my courses.

The fact remains, still: Though I believe firmly, and communicate explicitly, that all of my students matter equally, I've never bought the lie that I should expect equality from them in the classroom. I don't feel badly when a student fails to comprehend net ionic equations in chemistry; sometimes students choose not to invest their valuable and finite mental space on something that they see no use for after this year ends. I don't blame myself when a student hates "Ars Poetica" by Archibald MacLeish; some students are very practical, and simply don't like to spend their time pondering the myriad ways we have to define "art." My home state has decided they must learn these things; I'm not responsible for that decision.

I'm not suggesting you should settle for mediocrity in the classroom, and I'm certainly not saying you should ignore or overlook the students who don't click with your particular subject. In reality, by letting students know that I am perfectly willing to let them choose how invested they'd like to be in the subjects I teach—that I recognize they are not going to live identical lives, and therefore may have different outcomes in the course—I buy their goodwill.

This is vastly preferable to classrooms that demand their subjects be treated as vitally crucial to students' lives. These teachers, though often well-intentioned, tend to take one of two approaches to motivation: either they attempt to shame students into caring about the topic as much as the teacher does, or they attempt the sort of cheesy Hallmark-card manipulative motivation that teenagers see through immediately.

Every teenager knows hundreds of adults who live rich and meaningful lives without ever reading poetry. It would be insane for me to try to sell them on the idea that Shakespeare is vital to their happiness as a human adult. Every teenager knows hundreds of adults who've done quite well for themselves despite never taking physics. It would be ludicrous for me to attempt to scare or shame them into caring about kinematic equations.

My classroom takes this approach instead: I absolutely love what we do in here every day. I find value in knowing these things, and I've chosen to give my life to this. But there are many other people who love different things. If this makes you happy, I'm here to help you get better at it. If you see this as a practically wise investment in your future, I'm here to help. If you think this is a waste of time, I'm not going to try to force you into it, because I recognize that all of you are going to lead different lives—lives that matter equally, but that will not look equivalent in reality.

I saw a joke on Twitter a couple of years ago that I love to tell my students: A middle-aged economist and his non-economist friend are walking through a city one night when they pass the symphony. Upon hearing the music, the friend says, "You know, I've always wanted to learn to play an instrument." The economist immediately replies, "Apparently not."

(I didn't say it was a great joke.)

Think about all the things you've ever learned in your life. You've never learned anything you didn't want to learn. You only learned the things you wanted to learn. That may sound extreme, but it's true. Anything you've ever learned, you've learned because you chose to. You learned to walk as an infant because you wanted to get places without being carried. You learned to read because you wanted to know what was in the books you saw other people reading. When my son was four, he could work the same remote control that routinely stymied my wife. Why? Because he didn't want to be stuck watching his big sister's favorite shows forever. He wanted to watch what *he* wanted to watch.

If you want students to effectively learn something, you have to connect it to their innate curiosity and desire for autonomy—their inner will to learn the things that interest them. You have to create a scenario that increases the likelihood of their natural curiosity leading them to the choice you want them to make. That's easy if you're teaching really young children; they're naturally curious about almost everything.

However, as students grow into their personalities, they naturally become less interested in some classes and more interested in others. If you teach chemistry, the kids in your class who are interested in becoming doctors probably aren't terribly difficult to motivate. If you teach English, the kids who read novels at the lunch table probably lock into your lectures pretty well. It's easy to teach English to kids that like to read; it's easy to teach math to kids that like to solve puzzles. But how do you engage a student who just isn't curious at all about your subject? First of all, embrace the idea that *it's perfectly fine for students to be disinterested in your field.* There's a reason you became a history teacher instead of an accountant: because you were more interested in history.

So what do you do in the classroom for students that don't care about your subject? It turns out that the terrible joke I told earlier isn't entirely accurate. In reality, we also learn things all the time that we don't actually care about all that much. I dare say that back when you first started working, you probably weren't really excited about learning to file your taxes. I bet you didn't actually *want* to learn that particular skill.

But wait: of course you did. You had an intense desire to avoid prison. (If that's not true, I don't really know how to relate to you as a person.)

It turns out that we learn some things not because we are curious about the things in and of themselves, but because they are connected to other things we desire or are curious about. To satisfy your intense desire to avoid prison, you had to pay taxes. To pay taxes, you had to learn how to file them properly.

You may not necessarily want to learn to type quickly or code a website. But if you are interested in blogging, then being able to get your thoughts on the screen as quickly as possible in the style you desire may drive you to learn those secondary skills.

The human principle here is this: People are a bundle of wants, and often those wants are in conflict. When wants conflict, a choice is required.

PEOPLE ARE A BUNDLE OF WANTS, AND OFTEN THOSE WANTS ARE IN CONFLICT. WHEN WANTS CONFLICT, A CHOICE IS REQUIRED.

For some taxpayers, the desire to hang on to their time and money isn't as strong as their desire to properly file taxes; those taxpayers pay an accountant. For some bloggers, the desire to have a website look exactly as they envisioned it isn't as strong as their desire to save money and time; those bloggers settle for less-than-perfect websites or pay someone to build a website for them. These are all perfectly valid choices.

Of course, you already knew that adults made decisions about how to allocate their time and financial resources. What does this have to do with the classroom? First, you have to honor the choices your students make, as much as possible. Human beings have innate wants and needs that are specific to the individual. We honor the individual by not forcing their wants and needs to align with ours.

When I started teaching, I thought every student had to love my class. That's not necessarily a bad goal in and of itself; still, as much as we like to pretend otherwise, there really are "math people" and "English people" and "science people" and "art people." Although I believe the vast majority of human beings can be taught to perform competently (and perhaps excellently) in any endeavor, I've ceased thinking it's my job to force that on them.

Now, I tell students something like this: "I'm reasonably bright and hardworking. I could do anything and work anywhere. But I love literature. I love it so much I spent four years of my life learning to talk about it and earning a piece of paper that let me have this job. I love it so much that I have chosen to spend my time working in this classroom, talking about these books and poems and plays. I hope you'll love it, too. But if you don't, that's okay. It's not going to hurt my feelings. I don't understand why my son loves some of his video games; I'm sure some of you don't understand why I love Flannery O'Connor. But you get to be who you are in this room. So I promise to treat you guys who don't love literature with just as much respect as those of you who do, and I promise that together we will get you the credit you need to earn a diploma in this state."

(I did one more thing to make sure as many students as possible would love my class. I added a science and math certificate to my English certificate, so now I get to connect with three kinds of people instead of just one.)

What I've found is this: when students become aware that I'm perfectly fine giving them space to *not* love my class, they start trying to *figure out why I love my class*. I don't lie to them and tell them the quadratic equation is a crucial component of their future well-being as adults; I just let them see that I enjoy solving interesting problems, and I hope one day they will, too. I don't tell them you can't have a soul and also hate poetry; I let them see me fight back tears (every single time, dang it!) when we read "Those Winter Sundays."

And this part is crucial: I show my interest in what interests them. I let them see that a math nerd like me is also interested in talking about baseball games and prom committees.

Of course, I'm not actually interested in prom committees. No one but the prom committee is. But I make the choice—the human choice—to be interested in some topics not because of the topics themselves but *because my students are interested in them.*

Good teachers model the principle that most things are interesting because most things involve people, and people are always interesting. One of the best teachers I ever worked with used to say,

"Teach students to approach the world with open hands instead of closed fists."[1]

Closed-fist teachers start class by saying, "Okay, be quiet so we can start this lesson right now." But what they're actually saying is "I am only interested in what I came to do today, and whatever you are talking about is less important than that." Open-hand teachers start class by saying, "Thanks for being here today. Anybody got anything interesting to talk about before we get into act 2 of *Macbeth*?"

In fact, I keep a poster in my room that says, "Thank You for Being Here," just to remind me to start my classes by telling the students that. Early in the year, the new kids always say the same thing: "It's not like we had a choice." But I remind them: "Of course you did."

They could have skipped. They could have dropped out. They could have faked an illness. They could have shown up in body but checked out mentally. I want them to know that I value every single minute they choose to walk in my room and talk about chemistry and physics and poetry with me. Because until they recognize that learning is a choice, they won't really learn.

So how do you make that work in your specific class? I can't answer that question in a way that will work every time, but here are some potential questions you may want to push your less motivated students toward:

- What is it like to be a person who can converse intelligently about many different topics?
- What is it like to be prepared for the ACT?
- What is it like to legitimately have all college/career options open?
- What is it like to not worry about my grades?
- What is it like to impress my parents with something I learned at school?
- What would it be like to never have to worry about money?

---

1   Hey, Mrs. Tipton-now-Davis!

- What would it be like to be the smartest person in a room?
- What would it be like to not be scared by my next test?
- What would it be like to think of myself as a wise person?

There are plenty of other questions that might work. The point is that master teachers don't just deliver content; they figure out how to make the students curious about the content, which is a sales job. The student must believe that learning the material is in their own self-interest, so they will choose to step into the process of learning of their own free will.

Learning happens best at the intersection of curiosity and autonomy.

HUMAN HOMEWORK

1. Make your own "Launch Pad" poster and share it with students. Take the time to let them see where students have landed once they've left your classroom. Or, even better, give the class a project to create a survey that collects alumni data and figure out the best way to present their results.

2. Begin hosting weekly Career Conversations. I've just begun doing this recently. Once every month or so, I have an alumnus, parent, or community member come in for a short Q&A on what they do. The key to its success is this: no one has to come. I have students register ahead of time so I know how many are interested in freelance graphic design (to use this week's example). I have a script of eight to twelve standard questions, and then we turn it over to student questions. This is one of the best things we've done to help students understand the wide variety of jobs that are available to them outside of the standard four-year-degree model.

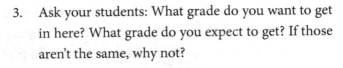

3. Ask your students: What grade do you want to get in here? What grade do you expect to get? If those aren't the same, why not?

4. If you didn't use the "What is School For?" graphic from the introduction, go back and do that now.

5. Have students complete the sentence "I want to be a person who . . ." with ten to fifteen different endings. Then, for each entry, have them finish the sentence "To make that happen, I'll need to . . ." And talk to them about your own answers to those prompts.

6. If you're not familiar with it, look up the Sudbury Valley School method, and ask yourself: How could I incorporate some of these principles into my classroom? My school? For example, my school isn't ready to even begin considering a widespread Sudbury approach, but we've started with one assignment. Each junior and senior, every year, is responsible for a nine-page paper on a topic of their choosing. The only requirement is that it be something worth discussing for nine pages. Each May, they assemble around the gym, and we open up the building for anyone—parent, student, alumni, community member—to walk through, listen to their three-minute summary, and ask anything they want. And this year, we've changed one of our bulletin boards to ask two questions: What do you want to learn about? What do you want to learn to do? Thus, next month, I'll be doing a three-day seminar to explain to a roomful of seventeen-year-olds how to buy insurance and file taxes, because many of them posted that on the board in the first week it was up.

FOUR

HUMANS LEARN AND HUMANS THINK

*H*umans learn and humans think. They're not the same thing. Humans think all the time without actually learning anything. We bought a new house when we moved to my current school. I'm not sure who designed this house, but the living room has ten separate light switches. We've been there for three years, and every single time I want to do anything involving living room illumination, I have to stare at all four walls and think about which switch I need to flip. I estimate in three years I've spent a combined six weeks staring at light switches.

I spend a lot of time in the dark. Because although I *think* about those light switches literally every single day of my existence, I still haven't *learned* them.

Really good teachers understand the difference between these two verbs. Inefficient, ineffective teachers assume they can be used interchangeably. I'm not suggesting it's necessarily bad to get your students thinking, just pointing out that thinking doesn't inevitably lead to learning. In fact, there are four different directions the student can go from "thinking":

1. They can learn the thing you want them to learn. This happens to me when I read new, challenging books about education.

2. They can learn nothing. This happens when I stare at the light switches. I just can't fathom dedicating any of my valuable remaining neural connections to codifying my light switches.

3. They can learn the thing you *don't* want them to learn. Who among us has not instituted a new classroom policy, only to realize three days later that we've incentivized some behavior we didn't mean to? I once got very progressive and told students that since my primary concern was that they learn the material, they could retake tests until they learned it. This created a never-ending cycle in which the study guide was ignored, the first test effectively became a study guide/practice test, and all future tests were endless incremental steps toward an eventual, inevitable perfect score. Though my goals were noble, my decision was impractical and impossible to implement. I also burned through twenty times as much copy paper as any other teacher that year.

4. They can wind up with more questions than they started with. This happens when I think about why God invented wasps.

As a teacher, I spend a lot of my time worrying about the difference between learning and thinking. I used to have my pre-algebra students complete thirty problems a night. They had to think a lot about the problems. Using the Four Directions framework above, here are the four outcomes I got, ranked from best to worst:

1. Some students learned the material I wanted them to learn.

2. Some students wound up with more questions than they started with. This can be good: "I see that dividing by a fraction requires flipping it over and multiplying, but why does that work?" Or this can be bad: "My mom works these problems out a different way than the book. Are all you adults

just making up math however you want? Or does this make any sense at all?"

3. Some students learned nothing. Looking back, I blame myself. I, the person responsible for helping them learn pre-algebra, had sent them away from my presence to do their learning. If they had a question about the problem at 8:47 p.m., I wasn't around to help them through it. So they would show up either with the work undone or with it done wrong.

Some students learned the wrong thing. What's worse than learning nothing? I'll tell you what: It's when a student uses the Magic Internet Answer Machine to generate the correct answers without having the faintest clue why they were right or how to replicate the process. They got what they were after (the homework grade), but I didn't get what I was after (mathematical comprehension). That's how you get a class full of students with perfect homework grades who somehow never demonstrate competency on an in-class assessment.

Treating students like human beings requires a willingness to carefully and clearly distinguish between thinking and learning, and to make sure that the classroom prioritizes learning. The good news is this: every human being that enters your classroom comes pre-loaded with all the software necessary to turn thinking into learning, as long as the right incentive structures are in place.

EVERY HUMAN BEING THAT ENTERS YOUR CLASSROOM COMES PRE-LOADED WITH ALL THE SOFTWARE NECESSARY TO TURN THINKING INTO LEARNING, AS LONG AS THE RIGHT INCENTIVE STRUCTURES ARE IN PLACE.

As I said earlier, by the time my son turned four years old, he could already work the remote control by himself. Think for a moment about all the ideas that he had to master to reach the simple end point of singing along to *Max and Ruby*. Since he could operate the remote, I have to assume that, even at his young age, he was capable of wrapping his tiny mind around an impressive list of concepts ranging from the fairly simple to the almost ludicrously abstract. Here's a short, off-the-cuff list of those concepts:

1. He understood cause and effect and expected the universe to be a consistent and logical place, since certain buttons always caused certain outcomes.
2. He knew his numbers, since he knew pressing 2-9-8 would pull up the Noggin channel.
3. He knew his letters and was on the way to reading independently, since he was able to find *Max and Ruby* in the DVR queue by himself.
4. He reasoned, since his rationale for finding *Max and Ruby* was that he knew it started with *M* ("M-M-Max"), and he could use process of elimination to weed out all the *M* shows that didn't feature his favorite annoying rabbit.
5. He recognized that a single device worked in multiple contexts, since he understood that he could use the same remote to watch old *Max and Ruby* episodes that I use to watch live football.
6. He was capable of memorizing a fairly complex sequence, since he could make a single remote operate both the TV and the DVR.
7. He understood that the universe is subject to invisible forces, since there's no concrete physical link between the remote and the devices it operates.

8. He was at least dimly aware of the second law of thermo-dynamics, since he would ask for new batteries when the remote didn't work, rather than assume the TV was broken.
9. He was capable of making abstract choices, since he alone decided whether he was in the mood for *Max and Ruby* or *GI Joe* or *Phineas and Ferb*.

Think about that list for a moment and think about how analogous it is to many of the skills that are routinely demanded of high schoolers. Can you perform this list of steps to solve for x? Which poem do you like more and why? What's the next number in this sequence? Why did World War II happen? How do we find the pH of a solution? What's the difference between weight and mass?

I'm not saying Jack Tyler could elucidate the things he understood at four years old; I'm merely observing that, on some level, he understood these things or was at least aware of their existence. I'm saying that my son had some thoughts, and those thoughts translated into learning.

And my son was not brilliant; he may turn out to be one day, but at four, he was fairly typical. We are talking about a child who sometimes used peanut butter as hair gel. At that age, he was a normal, reasonably inquisitive child. And this fairly average human (like many, many others) taught himself to operate a device that routinely frustrates his mother, a professional pharmacist with a six-year degree.[1]

Keep thinking and learning separate in your head. That's the "what." But how do you ensure that they're learning instead of just thinking? The "how" is easy, as anyone with children knows. Humans learn by doing five things:

1. Observing: Watching other people do something, reading about it, listening to a lecture, looking it up on YouTube.
2. Asking questions.

---

1 Who is also much, much smarter than I am. And beautiful. Hello, dear!

3. Giving it a shot.
4. (Probably) failing on your first try.
5. Asking questions about what went wrong.

It turns out, whether you're a four-year-old trying to watch *Phineas and Ferb* or a surgical intern trying to repair intracranial blood vessels, those are the four steps necessary to learn anything at all.

Notice that step five assumes it's likely that something went wrong. Failure, it turns out, is perhaps the most critical and memorable part of the learning process. This is why I refuse to obsess over my children's grades, or even look at them very often: a kid who never fails at anything, by definition, hasn't learned very much. They've just figured out how to do school.

In fact, I once asked four-year-old Jack how he learned to work the remote. His answer: "Umm . . . I mashed the buttons, and I figured it out."

So, I asked him, "If you couldn't make the remote do what you wanted, what did you do?"

"Umm . . . I went and got somebody to show me."

It's not complicated.

Here's how "homework" usually works for me now. Sometimes I hand students a set of problems and say, "We're going to be doing these in class tomorrow, so if you want to look them over tonight, feel free." Sometimes I hand them the problems with all the answers and say, "If you want to be sure you know what you're doing, try a few of these and check them against this answer key. If you're confident that you know what you're doing, there's no need to do all of them. As long as everybody's confident, we'll move ahead tomorrow."

I have a simple rule: I try to never give more work than they can finish in their spare time during the school day. Because I want them to have access to the same instant feedback from me that Jack got from his big sister about the remote. I want to make sure I'm available at the crucial moment when *thinking* can turn into *learning*.

This also affects the curriculum I choose. For physics, I prefer to use the online textbook from the Physics Classroom.[2] I love it because all of the answers are already there. When I assign work, I'm not asking students to come up with the answer. It's already on the screen. What I'm asking is for students to verify that they understand how the author arrived at the answer. When I'm not teaching a course that has correct answers already available in the text, I often post the Amazon link to the teacher's version of the book, so that students know how to track it down. Or I order a few extra copies and leave them scattered around my room.

In all of this, I'm creating opportunities to explain to students a crucial point: *This class is not about getting the right answers.* Anyone can copy the right answers from a book or a screen. In fact, I'm going to make it easy for you to do so, instead of fighting you on it. Instead, this class is about learning *how to get to those answers.*

Do some students copy answers anyway? Of course. But by making it easy for them to copy answers, and by openly discussing why I structure work the way I do, I make it much easier to hold them accountable for their eventual failure: "Well, you made perfect scores on every homework assignment, and you never asked a question about this chapter. Yet you made a 42 on the test. Why do you think that happened?"

This is particularly important in middle school, and for students who have learned (inevitably from their parents) to value the number on their report card more than the knowledge they've learned.

This works a little differently in English classes. For starters, I almost never use the "Read the story and answer the questions" model that permeates so many literature courses. In my experience, the questions that get written are either so basic that they're easy to

---

copy or guess the answers to, or they require such complex responses that it's not reasonable to expect a teacher to effectively evaluate thirty sets of answers.

Instead, my English classes are fairly repetitive. We read something interesting. I ask students how they feel about it: Was there anything they loved? Hated? Are they confused about anything? Did they find themselves nodding along with anything?

Then I explain what I know about the "why" of the work: What in this author's life, and in the cultural moment that produced it, led to the thing we just read? How does this connect to the bigger human story?

Of course, we learn some vocab and literary terminology along the way, but I'm very open about the fact that these things are completely secondary. We're not reading *The Remains of the Day* so that we can define what the term *unreliable narrator* means; we're reading it because the cost of failing to be honest with ourselves is a tragedy of the human experience, and everyone experiences that to some degree. We're reading it because if I can convince students to be unflinchingly honest with themselves, they'll avoid the hurt that Stevens, the protagonist, imposes on himself. We're reading it to understand how to be better at being human.

To drive this home, I give tests under a model I've adopted from Robert Marzano (and you should read everything he writes).[3] I use three sections, which I've boringly named Type I, Type II, and Type III.

Type I is straight objective memorization, usually requiring one-word answers: vocab, who wrote what, which work goes into which era.

Type II is still objective, but requires a more involved answer: Why did John Proctor of *The Crucible* refuse to sign his confession? Why are the two characters in Donald Barthelme's "Game" underground?

---

3   https://www.marzanoresearch.com

Type III is as subjective as it gets: Montresor seals Fortunato up in a wall in "The Cask of Amontillado." Why did he do it, and what would it take to make you do something like that? Why would you (or wouldn't you) date Editha from the William Dean Howells short story? Is Mark Twain's "War Prayer" offensive to soldiers?

There are really no right answers to Type III questions, and they're worth three to six times as much as Type I questions. It's routinely possible on my tests to skip every Type I question and still make a B by getting most of the Type IIs right and answering the Type IIIs effectively.

That's "what" and "how." Let's talk about the "why."

Why did Jack Tyler learn? Simple: Because he wanted to. Jack Tyler learned to work the remote because he didn't like relying on his big sister; it turns out, when she worked the remote, we watched a lot of *iCarly*, which he hated. It really is as ludicrously, stupidly simple as that. I've never learned to ride a unicycle or train a sled dog. You know why? Because it doesn't seem like any fun to me.

That's why I build my English tests the way I do. The message I'm sending is this: "You may have been led to believe that the reason we read stories and poems and plays is so that we will know the facts of what happened in them. That is not true. We read stories and poems and plays because they help us think about what it means to be us, in our own skin, on this planet. If you leave my classroom knowing a thousand literary terms, but no wiser about what it means to be human, I have failed. So I will build the class to incentivize deep thought and minimize meaningless memorization."

After twenty years in the classroom, I've decided the job of a teacher is much simpler than we allow ourselves to believe:

Step One: Let students fail their way toward learning the things they are motivated to learn.

Step Two: Try to motivate them to learn the things you think are important. (It should be noted that step two is optional.)

There is no step three. There is no backup plan. They are going to learn what they want to learn, and nothing else. If they don't instinctively want to learn it, or someone can't motivate them to want to learn it, they won't learn it. And certainly, nearly 100 percent of them will eventually realize that our society is organized in such a way that they are forced to submit at least enough to pass their courses.

But is that what I want? Do I want students who walk into my classroom the way I walk into the DMV: frustrated that they have to be there at all, and a little bit angry at the fact that they're being coerced to do something against their will?

I don't want that. It's important that students learn, but it's even more important that they *choose* to learn, and it will become increasingly important as an online world causes the available educational "delivery vehicles" to proliferate—Khan Academy and Edgenuity and Lambda School, etc. Perhaps—just perhaps—we should stop worrying so much about getting them ready for college, start treating them a little more like four-year-olds, and watch them learn the things they already want to learn.

Build incentive structures that turn thinking into learning.

HUMAN HOMEWORK

1. For a few assignments this week, use the Four Directions framework to consider the ways the assignment could turn out: As written, what behaviors might this assignment incentivize? Use that evaluation to tweak the assignment for maximal impact. Over time, it will become unconscious, and you'll save yourself plenty of time and energy that you would otherwise have wasted.

2. Ask your students to distinguish the difference between thinking and learning. "Waste" a class day talking it out and creating a shared vocabulary.

3. Ask your students how they learned to do something when they were younger: work an iPad, buy a candy bar, make slime. Use the opportunity to help them see that mental struggle is universal, desirable, and effective.

4. Ask your students: If you could learn anything in the world this semester, what would it be? Then create space and time for them to actually learn it. No matter what class you teach, there's value in communicating to students the idea that learning has value in and of itself, whether it connects to your particular field or not. If you're creative, you can usually find a way to connect the two. I've stopped putting anything but the most minimal topical restraints on final papers in my English courses—so I get to verify that students can generate a paper in MLA format while reading about the things that matter to them. This year topics included things as diverse as the history of stringed instruments, the efficacy of the electoral college, possible reasons for the divorce rate in America, commonalities in the childhood experiences of serial killers, possible causes of and treatment options for sleep paralysis, and more!

FIVE

HUMANS SMILE

They tell you a lot of things in teacher school. Unfortunately, a fair number of them are counterproductive to the actual practice of teaching students. I don't think it's intentional; it's just that they have to fill up four whole years of your time preparing you for the job, when anybody who's good at it knows you can actually only learn it one way: by trying to do it, doing it imperfectly, figuring out what went wrong, and trying again.

One of those unhelpful things is "Don't smile until Thanksgiving." I cannot tell you the number of times I have heard or read this awful old trope in communication to new teachers.[1] I used to keep a running count in one of my desk drawers; I quit counting once I reached triple digits.

Think of your favorite teacher from school; now think of the famously angry teacher at your school. Make a mental note that those two people are almost never the same. It turns out that a Venn

---

1 Though, to be fair, I never heard this one in teacher college—but I've heard it at every job since.

diagram of excellent teachers and angry teachers does not have a tremendous amount of overlap.[2]

There's a reason for that, and it (like so much of this book) is not complicated. You see, angry and miserable people are not fun to be around. Telling new teachers to not smile until Thanksgiving is the school equivalent of hiring a carpenter but refusing to let him use a hammer. Your sense of humor is your most powerful asset, because most humans like to laugh.

Joy and humor are universal to all human beings. Some students hate math. Some students hate to read. Some students hate sitting still. Literally no people hate laughing. Remember, all teaching is dependent on relationships, and laughing together is an important component of making them realize "This teacher is a person like me, with emotions like me—not a grammar robot."

So, what do you make them laugh at?

YOU MAKE THEM LAUGH AT YOU. Tell them stupid stories. When you mess up, laugh at yourself and make it okay for them to laugh at you. If you run copies and the copier staples the wrong corner, don't re-run them. Take them to class and do what I do. Hand them out, and apologize: "These are stapled wrong because the copier routinely outsmarts me. My career score against the copier is 176–787 in favor of the copier." This is a stupid joke, based on the fact that I am a person who is routinely defeated by basic technology. But here's the thing: feeling flustered and frustrated is a necessary part of how we learn.

My geometry students have legendary videos of me freaking out over the smartboard. There is a certain sequence of keys that makes it reset every single time. I have no idea which sequence it is. So, about

---

2 One notable exception: I had a physics lab in my second round of college that was run by a perpetually angry, frequently drunk Russian expatriate. He was freakishly smart and provided highly entertaining and memorable instruction, as long as you weren't the current object of his wrath.

every third week, I accidentally hit them in the middle of class, and the machine freaks out. Or Marvin, our Apple TV, spontaneously loses its connection to Mindy the MacBook, and I begin throwing markers at it while verbally abusing the machine. They absolutely love it.

Why does this work for me? It's actually pretty simple.

When we learn anything, there is a pretty long period of time when we don't yet fully understand the thing we're in the middle of learning.[3] For a student, this means that a significant portion of the day consists of them worrying about looking clueless. Most teenagers, trapped in the perpetual high school war for status, hate that embarrassment more than anything else on the planet. As teachers, of course, we try to tell them that failing to fully understand something doesn't in any way make a student "dumb," and that some moments of mental struggle are inevitable in learning any new skill.

But the fact remains: your students are still, very likely, worried about it. And if they're worried about looking lost, letting them know that you have that feeling, too—even if you wouldn't express it quite that way—is a particularly effective classroom tool (especially if you're like me and have that feeling routinely). It's even helpful to use those moments to explain that there's no reason to "feel dumb" simply because you don't yet understand something. After all, literally no babies enter the world knowing how to walk, yet all of us would assume that someone calling a crawling baby "dumb" is a monster. Our vocabulary may be different from that of our students, but we can still convey that we often share their experience of feeling inadequate to the learning tasks set before us.

The best way to leverage that common experience is through humor. When we choose to laugh, we are teaching students that joy

---

3 In fact, I just read a tweet from Shane Parrish (@farnamstreet) that said this: "Trying and struggling looks like incompetence right up until the moment it looks like success." That will be prominently displayed on my wall as soon as I can get to a printer.

is possible, even in the middle of frustration. We are teaching students that there is nothing to be embarrassed about when you occasionally feel foolish. Mistakes are universal, and there is no reason to feel alone in making them.

A short list of embarrassing things I have done in my career. Each of these I have openly discussed with students:

Got my tie caught in the laminator roller, nearly choking myself out. (PRO TIP: When you pull back against the laminator, it tightens your tie and chokes you more.)

Got so frustrated about a call with a parent that I threw the thing I was holding against the wall. (The thing I was holding was my favorite coffee mug.)

Slipped on a wet rug—which caused me to fall against a concrete ramp, peeling the skin off my leg from knee to hip and absolutely destroying my pants. (This was in full view of an entire high school.)

Picked up another teacher's phone, thought, "Oh, Mrs. Davis left her phone in the gym," and then used my phone to call Mrs. Davis (whose phone was in my other hand) to tell her I had her phone. I was in the middle of leaving a voicemail before it hit me that I could hear my own message in my other ear. (If you've ever seen *Inception*, you'll have some sense of my disorientation.)

Blew out the seat of my pants yelling at a ref in the middle of a basketball game. (This caused me to coach the second half with a sweater tied around my waist—but only after the fans in the stands alerted me to the color of my boxers.)

Lost 3,492 coffee cups. I am legendary for wandering the halls with a haunted expression, seeking my last cup of coffee. (I once placed it in a file cabinet, shut the drawer when I found the file I needed, walked away, and found it a month later looking for another student's records.)

Punched a goat. At Disney World. Fairly hard. (I had valid reasons.)

Dove for a ball at basketball practice. Well, not quite "dove." More like "ran, while stumbling, headfirst into the wall." This resulted in a dislocated shoulder and permanently damaged AC joint. Sadly, the security camera footage has been lost.

Experienced a concussion at an open gym that knocked me out of school for two weeks and still affects my ability to come up with the right nouns when speaking.

Threw a basketball to a female referee *way* too hard, resulting in a *very* clearly communicated technical foul. (From her perspective, she firmly believed I threw it *at* her. Perhaps because I was screaming at the time.[4])

There are SO MANY MORE of these moments I could have included. I seem to attract them like some sort of embarrassment magnet. Since I have so many, I lean on them constantly. I use them to make sure students understand that I see myself as just another person with the same sort of flaws and frailties as them. I use them to share lessons I've learned from mistakes I've made. Sometimes, I use them just because it's been a rough week in physics and we all need a laugh.

No matter how I use my failure stories, finding the joy in my own less-than-stellar moments accomplishes a couple of things.

First, it frees up my students to be open about their mistakes. I am telling them: "Stop worrying so much about looking foolish. I've pretty much scraped the bottom of the embarrassment barrel, and I survived, so I imagine you'll be okay, no matter how you do in math class today."

Do you remember high school? Constantly trying to make everyone believe you have your crap together, all while feeling like

---

4   Okay, so I wasn't exactly throwing it *to* her. But I also wasn't throwing it *at* her. I was throwing it to her hard enough that I knew she wouldn't catch it, so she'd have to dodge it. But I threw it slow enough that she'd be able to. See? I had a whole logic to it. I was younger, and louder, and I am not proud of this. But I *learned from my failure*, which was the point of the last chapter. Right? Anyway, don't throw basketballs at refs.

a cyclone of confusion and incompetence? I don't want my students to be alone in that, so I relentlessly deliver this consistent message: "All of us—including every grownup from me to the president—are working without a script in life. This is all an ad lib, and every single one of us messes it up. Figure out how to chuckle and move on, or you're doomed."

Second, it reminds them that I am a person, and students are naturally curious about other people. When I tell a story about my children, my students imagine me as a dad. They realize I have obligations other than them. When I tell them a story about my wife, they ask how I met my wife. (Answer: First day of first grade. I'll pause while your heart flutters at the magical sweetness of our story.)

This stuff is not fluff. It matters immensely. Teaching—especially at the high school level—is relational. There are a few highly driven students out there who are all about the work and don't care to know anything about the person at the front of the room. Planning to build a career out of those students is a good way to unnecessarily minimize your chances of broad success.

There's another way to put your sense of humor on display for your students, and I think it is the most underused tool in teacherdom. We are blessed to live in the era of social media. I know that it is fashionable among some adults to rail against phones and tablets in this connected generation, believing that these things damage education and are fundamentally detrimental to education.

So it is immensely amusing for me to read a tiny bit of history and realize this trend: overwrought, grumpy grownups have confidently stated that every innovation of the past, all the way back to the beginning of recorded time, would surely be the end of civilization. (For proof, you might want to peruse the @PessimistsArc feed over on Twitter.)

People hated the telephone. People hated the television. People hated the printing press. People hated newspapers. People hated cable TV. People hated cell phones. People hated tablets. People hated the internet. People hated social media. And people will hate whatever comes next.[5] Remember: *When people with power hate emerging technology, it is usually about loss of control.* When you hear someone gripe about new technology, ask yourself:

a) what control is being lost,
b) who is losing it, and
c) why do they care?

My point is this: social media is not going away. Being a modern teacher who gripes about tablets and Twitter and TikTok is roughly equivalent to living in 200 AD and saying, "We don't need any of that newfangled paper. They memorized everything Socrates said, so they can do it for me, too!" (The irony, of course, is that you only know everything Socrates said because someone eventually wrote it down using technology that was brand-spanking new at the time.)

I've personally watched teachers fill the board with notes. Then, instead of putting them online or letting students take a snapshot with their iPad, they force the students to write the notes out long-hand. We call these people Luddites. Look it up if you're unfamiliar with the term.

Technology's connection to the purpose of the chapter—which, if you remember, was joy—is this: humor is the currency of social media. Your school is full of students tweeting and snapping and Instagramming and TikToking, and most of them are engaged in the relentless pursuit of laughter.

You could spend weeks trying to convince your students that you understand and empathize with them, that you are a flawed and frail human being like them, that you don't view yourself as other than them or more important than them.

Or you could tweet a thread about how you walked into the wrong restroom because the Walmart in your new city is a perfect

---

5　My personal favorite (from @PessimistsArc) is the early-twentieth-century fear that flying would give people "Airplane Face."

mirror image of the Walmart in your old city, and how your mistake caused a nice old lady to *also* walk into the wrong restroom, and how she became very confused when you sprinted in her direction yelling, "No, wait!" and how generally this is a metaphor for the human condition.[6] And half of your students would laugh with you about it the next day.

Your social media presence is an efficient way to put your personality and expertise—and, above all, your joy—out into the world. A quick tour of my Twitter feed tells my students a terrific amount about me: what I think matters, what I find funny, what my family life is like. Perhaps that makes you uncomfortable. Perhaps you don't want your students in your life quite that much, or perhaps there are other mitigating factors that prevent you from connecting with students through social media.

That's certainly your decision, but it's going to make your job harder than it has to be. All teaching is relational, and effectively the entire world is now online 24/7. I assume you are reading this book because you want to be exceptional, rather than merely efficient. So if social media isn't a vehicle for you, you're going to have to find some other method of stepping into the world of your students in a way that allows you to demonstrate to them that you enjoy laughing, and you don't take yourself too seriously. For me, that vehicle is Twitter.

It was on Twitter that one of my favorite authors, David Dark, described the philosophy of Daniel Berrigan in a way that captures the job of a teacher well: "The job is to ring as true and as truthfully as one can, in every human exchange, and to then let it go." Be loudly, obnoxiously, joyously human with your students. They'll notice the difference, I promise.

---

6   Yes. This also happened.

HUMAN HOMEWORK

1. Make a list of the most embarrassing moments of your life. Then start looking for ways to give students space and permission to laugh at these moments with you.

2. Ask yourself each night: What made me laugh today? Would my students find it funny? If so, write it down and look for ways to work that into your classes the next day.

3. Carefully evaluate the way you deliver content to your students, and ask yourself: Is this the most efficient way? Or do I do it this way because I'm afraid to relinquish control? Does this create space (and permission) for joy in my classroom?

4. If you teach by putting bullet points on a board and having students copy the bullet points on paper, just stop. Instead, try Seth Godin's method of making great presentations: https://seths.blog/2011/10/the-atomic-powerpoint -method-of-creating-a-presentation. And make sure you don't do any of the things he talks about here: https://seths.blog/2007/01/really_bad_powe.

SIX

HUMANS SCREW UP

*H*umans screw up. And it's not just the students. You're a human, too. You knew that, right? I mean, deep down, you're aware that you get things wrong constantly, aren't you? And I'll bet you forgive yourself pretty readily. I know I do. Otherwise, life would be pretty close to unlivable.

Stephen Covey has a succinct explanation for why we're so quick to forgive ourselves and so ready to judge our students harshly: "While we tend to judge ourselves by our intent, we tend to judge others by their behavior."[1]

I think that sentence should be glued to every classroom wall in America, because it explains why so many teachers let themselves get away with behaviors they would never tolerate from their students. It explains why some teachers rarely apologize for things their students see as glaring mistakes. And it explains why some students are genuinely confused when teachers attempt to discipline them for their *behavior* without taking the time to explore the underlying *intent*.

---

1 Stephen Covey, *The Speed of Trust.*

The last chapter was about turning your humanity into humor as a way to connect with students. There are less funny ways to be human, and they're just as useful, though they may require more vulnerability than some teachers are prepared to display. For example: I've reviewed the relevant statistics, and it turns out it's very likely that you aren't perfect.

If you're not perfect, then you've done something wrong like the rest of us mere mortals. And if you've done something wrong, then you should apologize. But here's the thing: Most teachers never do. Ever.

I am editing this passage while watching the remainder of another teacher's class. These are the students that didn't leave early for an athletic event. There are ten freshmen in the room with me right now. That's a combined ninety years of schooling. And I asked them, "How many times have you ever heard a teacher apologize for doing something wrong?"

They came up with four.

Ninety collective years in school. Each year was 180 school days. That's a combined 16,200 school days. Each day was (minimum) six hours long. That's 97,200 hours in the classroom. And they remember four apologies.

You reckon their teachers only made four mistakes in all that time? Even if they were off by a factor of 100, that would mean the class as a whole only heard a teacher admit to doing something wrong about once per quarter. Does it seem likely that this class had been blessed to sit under teachers of such unparalleled near-perfection?

No. Of course not. Their teachers, like everyone else, approached the world with this all-too-common fallacy: "*The things that I do wrong* are perfectly justifiable mistakes, given the totality of circumstances and the unique context of the situation. *The things that others do wrong* are bald-faced moral failings."

In America, our culture lives in fear of apology. We fear giving apologies, and, because we rarely hear genuine apologies, we are hesitant to trust anyone who apologizes too readily. You don't have to watch much of any political cycle to figure out that, no matter how egregious the error, humans seem hardwired to double down, justify, and explain away their mistakes in a way that removes all fault from themselves.

When it comes to school, I think we've made it far too easy for teachers to get away with never apologizing.

If you go to the corner market, and a cashier is rude to you, you can complain to the store owner or manager, and it is likely that the boss will weigh the cost of losing a customer against the benefit of backing his employee before rendering judgment. If your mechanic is rude, you're probably going to find another mechanic.

But what about at school? What happens when a teacher mistreats a student? Not in an abusive or violent way, but in a way that is simply ethically wrong? What happens when a teacher is rude, or irrational, or cruel for no good reason? The answer is simple: almost 100 percent of the time, the teacher gets away with it. What can the student do? If the student is in a system that grants tenure, the teacher often can't be fired or even really disciplined for that sort of misbehavior. And it's quite possible that the student will remain in the class of the untouchable teacher they complained about.

Given the logic of the situation, it's no wonder that students have learned to gripe *about* teachers instead of talking it out *with* teachers. And this is the system most of your students have been raised in; they have internalized the idea that teachers don't admit wrong and teachers don't apologize.

This is no better in many private schools; although private schools may not grant tenure and are often perceived as having more accountability to students and parents, the fact still remains that many teachers view students as inferiors rather than equals. In religious schools, this may be exacerbated by an improper understanding of what the pertinent Scriptures teach about legitimate authority.

Sadly, some religiously motivated educators actually use religion to justify a mentality that implies, "I am trying to save this student's soul, and that end justifies any means."

On the other end of the spectrum, some insecure educators in religious schools may fear that admitting error on their part may cause students to question the religion they represent. Like Danforth in *The Crucible*, they assert that "While I speak the words of God, I will not crack his voice with uncertainty." Or those in nonsectarian schools may believe that openly admitting their flaws will cause students to lose faith in them as authorities in the classroom. This leads to a false bravado that does far more harm than good.

To both groups, and everyone in the middle, and myself, let me reassure you: Everyone—including our students—is keenly aware that we are human and that we are imperfect. So stop faking it. It's not working anyway. No one is buying it.

EVERYONE—INCLUDING OUR STUDENTS—IS KEENLY AWARE THAT WE ARE HUMAN AND THAT WE ARE IMPERFECT. SO STOP FAKING IT.

My career changed the day I realized this. As a young teacher, I often made up for the fact that I didn't really know what I was doing by displaying a false confidence in my own abilities. I made up for my own lack of preparation at times by allowing myself to believe that I was extremely stressed out because I had so many very important jobs to do. And I allowed that stress to impact the way I treated people, then I justified my temper after the fact.

One day, I jumped all over a student who asked me to repeat something I had already said multiple times. And I mean I jumped *all over him.* I have a very laid-back personality, but the trade-off is that once my anger is engaged, it kicks in at 110 percent right away. I made it crystal clear to the offending student (and everyone in the room) what I thought of his lack of attention, his failure to care enough to take good notes, and his general approach to life.

One small detail, which I failed to note at the time, was that the student had actually checked in halfway through the class. He was a generally quiet student, sometimes slightly disruptive, not academically motivated at all. I had (wrongly) assumed that he had been there all along, not paying attention. In fact, he had not heard the previous instructions, and was just trying to catch up.

Do you think my outrage made him more or less likely to care about my class or my opinion of him in the future? In fact, my anger caused him to shut down so hard that he didn't even defend himself by letting me know he had come in late while my back was turned, which was, ironically enough, *exactly* how I had instructed the class to come in if they were late, to avoid interrupting a lecture. He just wrote me off as another irrationally angry adult. It was actually another student, mortified by the scene, who approached me at the end of class: "You know, he had just gotten here when he asked that question. He was literally sitting down and trying to figure out where we were in the book."

Imagine my shame. In four angry sentences, I had alienated a student, damaged my reputation with an entire class, and exhibited a temper that was sinfully out of proportion to the offense. I wanted to reverse time. Since that wasn't an option, I had only a few viable choices:

1. I could pretend nothing happened.
2. I could double down and insist I was right.
3. I could admit I was wrong, but justify it somehow. I've begun calling this tactic a "non-pology." It goes something like "I'm sorry I yelled, but if you hadn't screwed around

so many times before, I wouldn't have assumed you were
screwing around this time, would I?" (Once you see your
first non-pology for what it is, you begin seeing them everywhere in our culture, for they are legion.)

4.   I could tell the student I messed up, and that I was sorry. I
     could take ownership of my own mistake.

You know I'm going to recommend number four. But how do
you apologize properly to a student? I believe the apology should
always be as visible as the mistake. If your mistake was in a private
email, your apology should be. If your mistake was in front of a class,
your apology should be. I learned this lesson through trial and error,
and it has not let me down yet.

As for apologizing publicly, that can be played by ear a bit. Some
students who are naturally shyer may actually prefer a private apology, no matter how publicly you messed up. You'll need to know your
students well enough to gauge their specific needs in this regard.

In this case, I waited a day and met the student at the start of his
first-period class. I asked the teacher ahead of time if I could make
an announcement. She probably assumed it was about SGA elections
or something mundane.

I went up to the front of the class and said, "Guys, yesterday I let
my temper get away from me, and I shouldn't have. It was wrong. I
made a faulty assumption when a student hadn't actually done anything wrong. I want you all to know that I was wrong, and I'm sorry.
I wanted you guys to hear me apologize, because you all watched me
lose it yesterday. That's not who I want to be, and I promise I will try
harder to not make faulty assumptions that lead to temper tantrums.
I wouldn't let you yell at me; I shouldn't yell at you. I hope you'll
forgive me."[2]

---

2   This is, of course, how I remember it. I don't have a transcript, and I
    doubt I was quite this eloquent at the ripe old age of twenty-five.

Here's the thing I've learned since that moment: when you are this honest with students, you worry a lot less about your mistakes. And so do they. When there's room for both teachers and students to admit they're human and receive forgiveness, the classroom becomes a much more liberated place.

We cannot teach students to live boldly and risk mistakes if we don't also teach them how to fix it when they get something wrong. We do that simply by being human in front of them, modeling apology when we mess it up.

The "getting it wrong" part will come naturally enough. You don't have to plan ahead for that. Just make a note on your desk: *I need to extend grace today, because I will need to receive grace today.* That is a sentence I keep somewhere near my desk most days, to remind me to apologize often and forgive freely.

I apologize for everything these days.

I apologize to the entire class if a test goes off the rails: "I'm sorry, guys. The average on this test was only a 68.3. I usually assume a solid average for the class is 75 on a test. So, I must not have done a great job teaching this unit. If you have any questions, come see me and I'll do what I can to make sure you know the material and boost your score accordingly." This apology means that, when I decide a low test score is actually their fault, they'll listen to my critique, because they remember that I was willing to be just as critical of myself.

I apologize to parents, too. Sometimes, I do this even when the root of the problem is related to a student's behavior or choices: "I'm sorry I didn't get those makeup grades entered yet. I got a little overwhelmed with the start of basketball season, but I'll make sure this weekend I enter those nineteen late assignments." Being willing to bear the blame on the little things means when I do pick a line in the sand to fight over, the parent may remember my track record of being accommodating.

I will even apologize to the student for their own behavior: "I'm really sorry you're having trouble settling down and paying attention.

I want you to know that I care about you enough to teach my guts out for you, no matter how long it takes you to get through Algebra II." What did I just do? Did I communicate to the student that he might not pass the course? Yes. Did I identify that outcome as a potential result of his own choices? Yes. Did I do it in a way that actually makes me look like the good guy? Somehow, yes.

Behind all of this apologizing is a simple concept: being openly human works. Think about the teachers in your school. Now fill in the blank: "_____ can never admit it when they mess up." In most schools, the name in that blank is also the teacher most loathed by the student body.

You're going to screw up. Admit it, apologize, and be human for your students.

HUMAN HOMEWORK

1. "We judge ourselves based on our intent, and we judge others based on their behavior." Talk about this sentence with your students and commit to giving them the same benefit of the doubt you give yourself when you screw up.

2. The next time you have to deal with student discipline, resist the temptation to be efficient. Instead, refuse to make a decision until you truly understand the "why" and not just the "what." In very difficult cases, I often tell a student that I'm going to spend the evening thinking about it before I make a decision. That gives me the chance to go home and—on paper—clearly lay out exactly what the problem is, what potential consequences are on the table, and what message is likely to be conveyed by each particular consequence. At times, I've even told a student to check their email at a specified time that evening, so that they could respond to any

follow-up questions I had before I made a final decision. It's amazing how much more willing to accept a disciplinary decision some students are once they truly believe that you're not just reading from a pre-written script.

3. Ask yourself: When is the last time I genuinely, truly apologized to a student for something? Or, even better, keep a notebook or file specifically dedicated to documenting these apologies, so that at the end of each year you can review mistakes and plan to minimize them moving forward.

4. Start identifying "non-pologies" when you see them. In fact, teach your students the word, and they'll help hold you accountable, too!

SEVEN

HUMANS HAVE CONFLICT

get it all the time: "Look, this empathetic, touchy-feely stuff would be great if all the kids were good kids. But I have twenty-nine in the room at a time, and some of them are only there to cause problems." And you're right: some of them *are* just there to cause problems. But building your classroom technique around the small percentage that are dedicated to derailing your lessons is like refusing to fill your car with gas because you've got one tire that makes an annoying noise.

Handle the routine maintenance of your classroom, get the majority of students in your corner, and a lot of the squeaky wheels will begin to sort themselves out when they recognize their hold on you is broken.

But what do you do when they don't come around? Because not all of them will. Human history is a long saga of warfare, much of it driven by a small chunk of humanity determined to fight no matter the circumstance. And your classroom each year is just a 180-day sample of that history.

So, what do you do when conflict emerges?

Let me level with you: I'm not that bright or inventive. Like any good teacher who's spent twenty years in a classroom, I've stolen a lot of ideas. Some of them, like "Thank you for being here," I can't even remember where I first heard.

But when it comes to conflict management, I can tell you exactly where I got the ideas. My most effective tools for classroom management come from Jim Fay's fantastic book *Teaching with Love and Logic*. I encourage you to buy this book and read every sentence in it. Much of that book informs my classroom approach; I do not exaggerate when I say it changed the course of my teaching career. In fact, I just bought a copy of it for every teacher at my school.

So, I trust that Mr. Fay will let me get away with this chapter on the assumption that at least a few of you will go buy his book as a result. (If you do, please email me a copy of your receipt so I can cite the sales in any future court cases.)

Any student in the world that's semiconscious has figured out what your rules are and how to work them. These are the students that can make life a nightmare, if you don't have a plan to handle them. (That they find loopholes also serves as a stark reminder that fewer rules are better rules.) Your rule says, "No speaking out of turn," so they obnoxiously tap their pencil. Your rule says, "No going to the restroom without permission," so they ask twice a day. The school rule says, "No candy in class," so they bring in breath mints and eat them like candy, clearly begging you to engage the argument.[1]

First: ignore, ignore, ignore. It's tautological, but basic: Attention-seeking behavior seeks attention. When you give it what it wants, you will get more of it. Of the examples listed above, I would let the breath mints thing slide. If I had my druthers, I would never have a "no food or drink" rule in my classroom, since it is a fundamentally irrational rule, but you may well find yourself in a school that has instituted such a rule campus-wide.

---

1   And if that doesn't work, they go to Luden's cherry cough drops, which—let's just call it—are red Life Savers without the holes.

But the other two—constantly escaping to the bathroom and intentionally being disruptive—must eventually be dealt with. However, there are still some things to consider as you enforce classroom rules, whether the rules came from your own brain or from somewhere over your head.

THE FIRST PRINCIPLE: RATIONAL TEACHERS DO NOT ENFORCE A RULE MERELY BECAUSE IT IS A RULE.

At least, we don't tell the students that's why we're doing it. The most counterproductive thing adults say in the known universe is "Because that's the rule." If the only reason to enforce a rule is because it is a rule, we can make any rule carry the moral force of the Ten Commandments simply by codifying it into the school handbook:

1. No green on Tuesdays.
2. All calculus must be done left-handed.
3. Desks must face southwest.
4. Only vanilla pudding is allowed in the lunchroom.

If our only justification for enforcing a rule is "Because that's the rule," then any of those rules are permissible. And obviously all of those rules are nonsensical. We enforce rules because the rules mean something; good rules protect the rights of all students. Teaching students anything else about "rules" contributes to their belief that authority is arbitrary and capricious.

I like to get sort of Constitutional, to approach the enforcement of rules from a foundation of human rights. A student tapping his pencil obnoxiously is inhibiting the right of other students to learn free from unreasonable distraction. (Note, though, that if no other students have complained, this may not be true—which puts us back to "ignore it.")

A student that constantly attempts to go to the bathroom excessively *may be* a distraction, inhibiting the freedom of other students to learn; *on the other hand*, getting them out of the room may actually make the situation better for the rest of the class.

WE ENFORCE RULES BECAUSE THE RULES MEAN SOMETHING; GOOD RULES PROTECT THE RIGHTS OF ALL STUDENTS. TEACHING STUDENTS ANYTHING ELSE ABOUT "RULES" CONTRIBUTES TO THEIR BELIEF THAT AUTHORITY IS ARBITRARY AND CAPRICIOUS.

In either situation, there is a magic question that has worked for me in 100 percent of potential disciplinary situations. I say *potential* very intentionally. Any disagreement is potentially a disciplinary situation. But as a teacher, if I can keep it in simple "disagreement land," there's a lot less emotional charge to the situation. Once a situation veers into "discipline," it becomes more complicated by default.

Consider: one student wants to tap his pencil, and I don't want him to. This is (at the moment) simply a difference of opinion. The other student wants to go to the bathroom more often than I think he should. This is (at the moment) simply a difference of opinion.

PRINCIPLE NUMBER TWO: RATIONAL TEACHERS DO NOT CREATE CONFLICT OUT OF THIN AIR.

If a teacher barks, "Stop tapping that pencil right now!" then they have created a conflict out of thin air.

If a teacher spouts off, "You ask to go to the bathroom too much! Sit down!" then they have created a conflict out of thin air.

But what happens when I respond with a question? An open-ended question forces the student to work off-script. He assumes I will bark, or snap, or throw him out of class, or write him up, or whatever passes for "discipline" with other teachers he's experienced. I don't want him to run the program he's learned for ten years and initiate the "get back at the guy who just embarrassed me" sequence. So, I ask a question, as calmly as possible. It is always the same question, delivered as calmly as I can manage. Below, I've outlined a few potential responses and how I would handle them.

SCENARIO A: THE NIHILIST

My Question: "What do you think will happen if you keep loudly tapping that pencil?"

The Nihilist: "Probably nothing."

My Response: "Well, I've stopped teaching to point it out. So obviously it's not 'nothing.' But since you don't have any ideas, I'll try: let's say if you keep it up, I'm going to ask you to hang out after class so we can talk about how you can occupy yourself without distracting me. Will that work? Or do you want to try something else?"

Why This Works: I haven't yelled. I haven't taken his pencil away. I haven't done anything that he can perceive as anger or conflict. I have yanked the rug out from under him; it's likely that he has no script in his head for what to do when a teacher actually solicits his opinion regarding classroom behavior.

What Comes Next: If he stops, mission accomplished. If not, after class we talk. I simply explain that I wouldn't sit behind him at the movies and distract him, and I love my job so much that teaching for me is like going to the movies. I may be the first teacher he's known who admits to him that they love their job. It sounds idyllic, but I have rarely had this approach go wrong for me, and I've been using it consistently for over a decade.

SCENARIO B: THE KID WHO'S SEEN IT ALL

My Question: "What do you think will happen if you keep tapping your pencil?"

The Kid Who's Seen It All: "You'll probably [kick me out/ write me up/call my mom]."

My Response: "Well, I was actually just gonna say we could talk about it, because it's really not that big of a deal. But if you think that could work—sure, we can try that. You probably know what works for you better than I do. You got a deal. We will do exactly what you just said if you keep it up. Thanks for the input."

Why This Works: I haven't yelled. I haven't taken his pencil away. I haven't done anything that he can perceive as anger or conflict. In fact, I have told him that I was actually going to be more lenient than he's asking me to be. Plus, he named his own consequence—so when I do it (if he keeps the behavior up), there's no way he can justifiably be angry at me.

What Comes Next: It's simple. If he quits, problem solved. If not, I just do the thing he told me to do. And notice: now I'm negotiating with him as a peer, rather than bossing him as an authority. Occasionally, students will get angry anyway, but being able to tell a parent, "Ma'am, the whole class watched your son flip out while I calmly asked him how he'd like to solve the problem" sure makes the parent conferences easier.

SCENARIO C: THE CONFUSED KID

> My Question: "What do you think will happen if you keep that up?"
>
> The Confused Kid: "I don't know."
>
> My Response: "Oh, come on. You're a bright student. You crushed that quiz the other day. You've been in school for eleven years. Surely you have some idea. Give me a guess."

Why This Works: I haven't yelled. I haven't taken his pencil away. I haven't done anything that he can perceive as anger or conflict. In fact, somehow I worked a compliment into a disciplinary situation. And I'm pushing him to name his own consequence (see previous).

What Comes Next: If I can get him to name a consequence with a little prodding, I'm back to scenario B. If he won't, I use the plan from scenario A.

So what do I do with Bathroom Boy?

In this case, my question is a little more specific: "What do you think will happen if you keep missing class to go to the bathroom?"

This one is slightly different, because there's not really a disciplinary issue here. And remember: *Bad teachers create disciplinary problems out of thin air.* They do this by failing to distinguish between irrational behavior, inconvenient behavior, and immoral behavior.

Immoral behaviors include things like cruelty, defiance, assault, theft, and vandalism. Immoral behaviors exist when the student infringes on the rights of others (whether they are teachers or fellow students).

Irrational behaviors include things like tardiness, excessive absences, leaving class, failing to turn in assignments, etc. Irrational behaviors exist when the student fails to recognize the logical consequence of their decision, or seeks to be insulated or protected from those logical consequences.

Inconvenient behaviors include things that may complicate the classroom but aren't really the fault of the student. A student with a sensory issue may tap their pencil as a coping mechanism. A student with a medical issue may have a legitimate need to visit the restroom three times as often as their classmates. A student who's consistently tardy may be dressed and ready to go on time each morning, yet have no adult in the home responsible enough to get them to school before the bell. The key takeaway here is that an effective teacher never defaults to assuming a student's behavior is immoral; instead, effective teachers recognize that we often can't distinguish between different kinds of behavior without asking some questions to ensure we understand why a student is doing what they're doing before we react to it.

The Bathroom Boy example is illustrative. There is nothing fundamentally wrong with asking to go to the restroom. Everybody pees. I know, because my parents read a book about that to me when they were potty-training me.

Of course, it's possible (maybe even likely) that the student in this example is using the restroom as a way to escape a class he doesn't want to be in. (We don't have time to talk about this here, but let me briefly say that if students are constantly trying to escape your class, consider the possibility that the problem is your ability to plan and execute engaging lessons, and not the students themselves—and perhaps your efforts would be better spent solving that problem first.)

I could deal with this problem as one of morality: "You know this class is important, and it is wrong for you to constantly try to get out of it." And if I do that, I have drawn a line in the sand and essentially begged the student to cross it. I personally know a teacher who refused to let a student go to the bathroom, and the student wet himself in spite just so he could tell his mom about the horrible teacher who wouldn't let him pee.

Or, I could treat the student in good faith (again, open hands instead of closed fists) and assume he's telling the truth. What happens if I assume he really has to go? This frees me up to deal with the problem rationally instead of emotionally.

What does that look like in an actual classroom?

"Sure, you can go. But I notice you go during this time every day, and every time you go, we're working on a new geometry lesson. What do you think will happen if you keep missing geometry lessons ten minutes at a time? Imagine it's a month from now, and you've missed two hundred minutes of geometry. That's over three hours. That's three *Breaking Bad* episodes worth of time. Could you skip three hours of a TV show and keep up with the plot? If you skip three hours of geometry, will you be on track?"

Of course, the student may be a genius. Or he may not care about learning geometry. Or he may have a legitimate medical reason to visit the restroom. If the student's a genius, and he can make the grade while missing class for ten minutes a day, kudos to him. If he doesn't care about learning geometry, refusing to let him go to the bathroom isn't going to solve *that* problem. It's only going to create conflict out of thin air. And if he has a legitimate reason to visit the restroom, it's my job as the adult in the situation to help him figure out an alternate plan, like how we could cover the material he's missing out on.

Here's what I'm going to do: I'm going to let him go to the bathroom, every single time. First of all, remember that I don't generally run a classroom where I expect students to request permission to go to the restroom. But they still often ask from force of habit.[2] Others will simply tell me their intention on the way out the door. But whether they ask first or tell me on their way out the door, I still let it happen every time. By doing that, I'm communicating to the student the following message: "I believe you are in charge of your outcome in this class. And if you and your folks are happy with your grade, you can miss five minutes at a time every time you need to." I might even say that out loud to him at the moment, or in private later. If his mom calls to ask about the grade, I'm going to tell her, "He misses class for ten minutes most days to go to the bathroom." And if she doesn't like that, and asks me to keep him in class, guess who Bathroom Boy is mad at now?

Not me. I am Coach Adams, who believes in him and treats him with respect. I am on his side. He's not mad at me; he's mad at his mom. Should he be? Probably not. But my job is not to navigate the student's relationship with his parents for him. My job is to teach him geometry. And that's a lot easier to do when we're not arguing about his bladder.

Obviously, you'll have to experiment with this some on your own to find what works for you. But no matter how you phrase your student communication, remember:

1. Don't confuse immoral behavior or inconvenient behavior with illogical behavior.
2. Don't create conflict out of thin air.

---

2   By the way, a fun response to "Can I go to the bathroom?" is a deadpan "Not right there," followed by immediately turning away to proceed with whatever you were doing.

HUMAN HOMEWORK

1. Read *Teaching with Love and Logic* and (if you have children of your own) *Parenting with Love and Logic*. I don't get paid to endorse those; I just can't express to you how much positive impact those two books have had on my personal and professional life.

2. Make a list of the behavior that tends to derail your classroom the most often. Then, write out exactly what you're going to say the next time it happens. Game it out in your head, so that you're the only one with a pre-written script when the time comes.

3. Count it out: How many times do you remember raising your voice this month? For each one, write down how it might have gone differently if you'd used the methods espoused by *Teaching with Love and Logic*.

4. Walk into class one day and announce a new rule—the more arbitrary, annoying, and irrational, the better. Force the students to articulate what's wrong with the rule, then "waste" a day talking about why they're right, and why the other rules—the good ones—exist.

5. List the behaviors that bother you in your classroom, and sort them into Immoral, Inconvenient, and Irrational. Simply having them pre-sorted in your head can help you respond more calmly when something goes wrong.

EIGHT

HUMANS THINK BIG

I've been in a lot of schools. I attended one school, student-taught in three others, worked in three, and I've visited scores more. But one thing that baffles me at every school I've ever been in is this: so very few teachers walk around with books. I don't mean textbooks—I mean novels and works of nonfiction. It's as if something happens to some teachers; once they get in a position to teach other people, they just drop all their curiosity about the world and any interest in learning.

It's not all of them; I have been blessed to work with many voracious readers over my career. With those people, I've shared books and ideas almost constantly. On the other hand, I've also worked with people like the one who remarked, as I put the book I was reading on the lunch table, "Coach, you make *me* tired carrying that book around all the time."

The point is simple: it's patently irrational for teachers to be frustrated with students who don't like to learn if the adults they encounter in school don't like to learn. Rarely does a week go by in my classroom that some student doesn't look at whatever book I'm reading and ask, "What's that about?"[1]

Sure, sometimes we wind up spending half of a chemistry class talking about the potential large-scale effects of a minimum wage increase (*Economics in One Lesson* by Henry Hazlitt) or gender expectations in Elizabethan England (*Hamlet*) or statistics and distributions (*The Bell Curve* by Charles Murray and Richard J. Herrnstein) or the tension between faith and reason (*Educated* by Tara Westover[2]) or any other thing in the world that happens to connect to whatever book I'm currently reading. But that is a small, easy price to pay, and it is absolutely worth it to model to students that there are adults out there who are still fascinated by the world.

The biggest fear most teenagers have is that their brains won't know how to be adults by the time their bodies get there. By constantly reading and talking about books and blogs and news in front of them, I am signaling to them a very important fact: I don't know how to be an adult yet, either; I'm figuring it out on the fly like every other "grownup" in the world.

I'm also using my behavior to reinforce something I constantly say to my students: only boring people get bored. I've never been bored. I suppose, trapped in a cell with blank white walls, I might be forced to re-evaluate my position. But out here in the free world, with my phone that connects to the internet and Amazon ready to send books to my Kindle at any moment, I never run out of questions to ask or things that fascinate me.

In teacher school, professors talk a lot about the "teachable moment" or the "zone of proximal development," by which they mean that moment when something is starting to click with a student

---

1   In fact, I now keep a running Twitter thread of every book I read, so the students who follow me online see evidence that I mean it when I tell them that reading leads to a fuller life.

2   READ THIS BOOK, YO.

and all they need is a little nudge to learn a new thing or lock in a new skill. My point here is simple: quit assuming all the teachable moments will somehow connect to your particular course.

You're here to teach science or math or English, sure. But more importantly: you're here to model a thoughtful, intelligent, curious life. Laura Stokes, who did a fantastic job editing my thoughts into some sort of logical order for this book, has a great line on this point: "Adolescents fear that adulthood is stasis, and stasis is anathema to teenagers." Sadly, the employment satisfaction statistics referenced early in the book indicate that many students can't even look to their own parents to catch a glimpse of an adult who loves their own life. Though sad, this is a powerful lever for teachers, because it means that simply by letting your students see that life doesn't end when you turn thirty, and that your own life is still full of wonder, curiosity, and awe, you can inspire them to truly value the learning that they're capable of and the wisdom that's available to them.

The students I teach are naturally inquisitive, and they want to know more about everything. Today, getting ready to teach chemistry, I got asked my opinion on the president's most recent executive order. So of course I asked the students what they thought, and then I prodded their thinking to push them to consider alternative viewpoints, and I explained my thoughts on the issue, as well as the perspective of those who might disagree with me. Zero chemistry was learned. And it was a fantastic class.

Sometimes, they ask me something I don't have a clue about. One week in physics, a student was griping about a ticket they got the afternoon before, and out came the questions: "Coach, why do we even have speed limits? When did we start them? Who sets them?"

Dear. Sweet. Moses. What a blast we had figuring that out. I found a couple of ways to connect what we learned to the course material as we went. But much more importantly: I modeled how to do research online. I got to talk about the difference between a valid source of information and a rando running a sketchy blog from his mom's basement (or a genius running a brilliant blog from his mom's basement, for that matter). We got to talk about the structure of government (because we didn't have a federally mandated speed limit until the seventies). We got to talk about safety. We worked out the difference in reaction time between driving at 55 mph versus 75 mph. We talked about relative velocity. We talked about the difference between raw number and rate as we compared traffic fatalities by state and by decade. Most importantly, I told my students, without using these exact words, that their questions about the world were both valuable and answerable.

Will there be a day later where I can't afford to give up class time to discuss their questions? Sure. But by giving up some control when I can, I buy back the right to exert some control when I need to. To paraphrase Jim Fay (again): "Students are going to get some control of your class at some times. You can give a bit of it up to them on your terms, or constantly fight them as they try to take it on theirs."

And—if I'm honest—I also enjoy it when a class takes a turn I wasn't expecting. Shakespeare hasn't written any new plays, and balancing equations hasn't changed much in the last twenty years. Being open to taking an intellectual detour doesn't just benefit the students, it offers me a valuable chance to break from routine as well.

So when they ask a question that cracks the door to some big idea, I pounce. Whatever lesson I had planned that day is likely out the window. In an odd way, that's actually a positive (if unintended) side effect of the fact that the school year is now waaaaayyyyy too long. Because there are more days in the school year than I need to cover my material effectively, I'm free to ditch the plan from time to time to talk about the big stuff.

And so are you.

HUMAN HOMEWORK

1. Create a "What I'm learning" space at your desk. Keep a running tab in your room (or on Twitter, if you're on social media with your students) of the books you read, the movies you watch, the conferences you attend, etc. And, most importantly, *talk* to your students about what you're learning, why you're doing it, and how it's changing you.

2. Create a shared document that your colleagues can all use to post what they're reading, learning, and working on, and why. We generated several months' worth of spontaneous professional development last year, simply by setting up a Basecamp page for our teachers to list whatever books about teaching they had available in their classroom.[3]

3. Give each student permission to stop class completely once per semester to get any question answered, whether it connects to the course material or not. In my classes, I simply communicate to students that they should feel free to ask me anything at any time, whether it connects to the lesson or not. If you need more structure, consider a "Big Questions Box" that you draw from once a week, or take a timeout every Wednesday to ask students to write down the biggest question they have unresolved at the moment.

4. Make a list of the times you've had to fight students for control. For each one, come up with a way you could give up that control in smaller increments and on your own terms.[4]

---

3 Basecamp is free for educators!

4 If you're the sort that gets nervous about deviating from the lesson plan, consider taking an improv class, joining Toastmasters, or taking part in community theater as a way to develop your own ability and comfort level when it comes to spontaneous learning.

NINE

HUMANS LOVE

No one goes into teaching because they hate students. In fact, a survey in the UK found that 93 percent of teachers entered the profession because making a difference in people's lives was important to them.[1] Teachers arrive in their buildings, fresh out of college, with the best of intentions and the most idealistic hearts imaginable. Every one of us thought we would eventually have a *Dangerous Minds* or *Dead Poets Society* made about our career. Remember feeling that way?

Now, picture the adults you share your building with. (Or, if you're brutally honest with yourself, go look in a mirror.)

What happened? We need to think about it and think hard. The wires got crossed somewhere along the way, because a 2009 study of over four hundred thousand students found that *less than half* of them believe their teachers care about them as individuals.[2] A full 55

---

1   https://blogs.edweek.org/teachers/teaching_now/2015/10/survey
    _explores_why_people_go_into_teaching_in_the_first_place.html

2   https://www.educationworld.com/a_issues/chat/chat239.shtml

percent of those surveyed believed that their teachers didn't care if they were absent from school.

How can this be? How can hundreds of thousands of teachers somehow *accidentally* convince hundreds of thousands of students that we're just fine without them in our classrooms, and our lives will tick along just swimmingly whether they bother to show up or not?

Nightmare stories abound of the truly horrible teachers who say things like "I get paid whether you learn or not," but if you cared enough to read this book, that's not you. And anyway, I don't think they're actually the primary problem. (Although I've personally heard teachers say this, and I hereby deputize you to loosen the wheels on the rolling chair of any teacher you know who utters this abomination.)

The primary problem is the wholesale systematization of education. Systems and organizations can't love. The DMV can't love you, and neither can the post office or the movie theater. Love has to happen between human beings. Which means if you're not comfortable being human with your students—and letting your students be human in your classroom—you're never going to see great success in any classroom.

When I was hired for my second teaching gig, the athletic director interviewing me gave me one piece of advice at the end of the job offer: "They have to know you love them. If you can't tell them 'I love you' in a way they'll actually believe, you're dead in the water." I stayed in that school for sixteen years; just last summer I got to attend a former student's wedding, and my wife and I wound up hanging out in the hotel lobby with about a dozen former students from that school until two in the morning, laughing and reminiscing.[3]

Believe it or not, I am not a terribly emotional or outgoing person. I was less so back then, at twenty-two years old. My default state is analytical, and logical, and fairly cold. I am rarely happier

---

3   And, inexplicably, ordering $119 worth of Greek food and waffles around midnight.

than I am when I'm going through spreadsheets of data, just me and my numbers.

So this love thing was a challenge for me. But that athletic director was right. It took me a decade to fully grasp it, but until students feel loved by their teacher, their work in the classroom will always be limited by their natural ability and personal interest in whatever your subject happens to be.

Once they realize you love them, though . . . they'll run through walls for you. And to demonstrate love to them, you really only have to do two things: notice and communicate.

Grant Wiggins, longtime president of Authentic Education,[4] reported in one study that fewer than 50 percent of all students believe "my teachers really know me."[5] I did a survey of my own current and former students. Granted, it was a much smaller data set, but when asked "What quality is necessary to be an effective teacher?" 57 percent of respondents identified patience, understanding, or positivity as crucial traits.

This illustrates an important idea. In an awful lot of classrooms, the student-teacher relationship is adversarial by default. It's important to grasp that this is not an accident. At some point it was built into the design by people who may have meant well, but were the sort of people who agreed with things like the aforementioned lunacy "Don't smile until Thanksgiving." Love is not adversarial. Think about the last argument you had: Did you feel loved?

Flashback: I was sitting at lunch, listening to teachers complain about a particular class, thinking, "It's February, and I haven't had a problem out of that class yet. Not a glitch." So the next day, I asked the class this question: "Let's say—theoretically—I heard some teachers complain about you guys. And let's say—theoretically—that

---

4 authenticeducation.org

5 https://grantwiggins.wordpress.com/2014/05/21/fixing-the-high -school/

I thought that was weird, because we haven't had any problems in here. Can you guys help me understand that?"

Without hesitation, the very student who was the subject of much of the lunch table's ire spoke up: "It's easy. You don't treat us like we're all potential felons. You don't assume we're bad just because we're teenagers. You talk to us like we're people."

You must grasp this: The average experience of tens of millions of teenagers has been that many adults are impatient, stressed-out grumps who make arbitrary decisions without thinking about how those decisions will affect their students. And, shockingly, this pattern has not made them feel loved.

This isn't your fault, specifically (unless you've been one of those adults). It's just the nature of the beast we've built in American education. And although it's awful, it actually provides a giant lever you can use to differentiate yourself from other teachers. Quite literally, all it takes to set yourself apart, in a lot of places, is this: be nice. It's that cheesy, and that simple. But man, is it ever effective.

In practice, your first task is to start peeling that adversarial relationship away, simply by letting a few students know you've noticed something about them that mattered to you. (Another thing I learned from Jim Fay.)

To do this effectively, you don't need to become a children's TV host, dispensing meaningless, insincere platitudes. All teenagers have built-in BS detectors and will spot that a mile away. False praise is patently offensive to them, so don't try it unless you want to spend a lot of time undoing the mistrust it will create. But one or two well-placed, thoughtfully communicated "moments of notice" a day will overhaul your entire career.

An effective compliment needs to meet these criteria:

1. Sincere: Genuinely mean what you are saying. If you can't mean it, don't try to say it.

2. Specific: Make it about something concrete. Don't tell them, "You're a good person," or "I think you're witty." Tell them, "It's cool that you hold the door for the younger students," or "You always write at least one sentence in your papers that makes me laugh out loud."

3. Succinct: Spend too much time or enthusiasm praising the student, and it'll get awkward fast. In fact, you won't earn the right to do that until you've gotten their trust in a million other ways.

4. Spontaneous: Get it out in a natural way. Leaving class, passing in the hallway, chatting in the lunch line. Don't call the student to the front of the class to make a speech about how awesome they are. Think about the adults you know: The ones who crave that sort of public production are often ones that least deserve praise, right? The same logic applies here: If it feels like a student's primary motivation is a craving for public praise, they may not be the student you want to single out.

I cannot hammer this point home to you enough: the life of a teenager is continuously full of adults who are suspicious of virtually everything he does; a single adult noticing that a teenager is actually fairly awesome can be paradigm shifting. And once you achieve a critical mass of students that actually believe you like having them in your classroom—that you love them as human beings—your life as a teacher gets immeasurably easier.

Here's another pattern I've found: Noticing begets more noticing,[6] and more noticing begets genuine love. As I began communicating the things I noticed to students, relationships shifted. I began to notice more—both more things to admire about the batch of students I'd started with, and more students who had attributes I

---

6 To paraphrase a business truism: you make more of whatever you measure.

hadn't previously noticed. It became a habit. And as I noticed more, this spreadsheet-loving nerd started to grow a heart. I could tell my basketball team or my chemistry class, "I love you guys," and they believed me. And as I got comfortable talking that way to the groups I was in charge of, it got a little easier to say it to individuals.

ONCE YOU ACHIEVE A CRITICAL MASS OF STUDENTS THAT ACTUALLY BELIEVE YOU LIKE HAVING THEM IN YOUR CLASSROOM—THAT YOU LOVE THEM AS HUMAN BEINGS— YOUR LIFE AS A TEACHER GETS IMMEASURABLY EASIER.

And now, after years of building the habit, I can tell a student who's been sent to my office for discipline, "I love you, and because I love you, we're going to figure out how to fix this problem." And they believe me. They believe me because it's true.[7]

Do you know how much easier parent-teacher conferences are when the kid knows you love them? Try it.

---

7   Not only that: when I think about the few student or parent relationships that have really gone off the rails in my recent career, I can trace nearly every one back to a failure on my part to follow my own advice in this chapter.

HUMAN HOMEWORK

1. Spend five minutes writing about why you went into teaching, then take a five-minute break. When you come back, spend five minutes writing about why you go to work every day at this point in your career. Are the reasons the same? If not, where did they diverge? Can you put your finger on a moment or identify a pattern?

2. Make a list of one thing you could say to each student you teach to indicate that you love them. If you can't come up with anything for a particular student, brainstorm with some colleagues who also teach that student. Figure out how to get that sentence across to them in a way that will make sense to them.

3. Survey your kids: "What qualities make someone a good teacher?" Then figure out how to put those qualities on display in your classroom. (Even better: Have each student in your class teach something they consider themselves good at or knowledgeable about. When it's over, have the class evaluate the lessons to identify what traits and qualities showed up consistently in the most effective teachers.)

HUMANS CHEAT

*H*umans are going to cheat. Not all of them, and not all of the time. But if students are human beings, which is the (admittedly obvious) central premise of my entire career, and human beings lie, then it's definitely going to happen. How, then, is a teacher supposed to deal with this aspect of human nature?

Let's talk about how not to deal with it first.

Paradoxically enough, one excellent way to deal with cheating is to act as if you don't expect it at all. If you've been to school, then you remember the one teacher who didn't trust any students, ever. Every test was a giant production: "I need you to move all the desks at least nine feet apart, and everyone get their cover sheet out right now, and don't even *think* about cheating, because there is a separate version of the test for every student in the room."

I bet that teacher wasn't the reason you went into education.

Students know people cheat. Heck, most students know they've cheated themselves at some point. But nobody likes being treated that way. Remember, our goal is to teach students to approach the world with "open hands instead of closed fists," so we have to model the behavior we're asking them for.

The benefit of the doubt is an extremely powerful tool, and it's something we expect in our own lives. When we're denied it, we're likely to lash out. How do you feel, for example, when the cashier uses the counterfeit-detection pen on your cash at the grocery store? Or when you're asked for ID when using your credit card in your hometown? I bet you don't think, "Thank God for this brave store owner, establishing a policy to cut down on fraud and thereby minimizing my future costs at this establishment!" If you're anything like me, you feel 1) annoyance at the inconvenience and 2) anger at being told—in a decidedly unsubtle way—"I don't assume you're trustworthy as a person."

There are a few principles that have served me well in managing student behavior on assignments. First, I'm intentional about establishing a classroom culture that incentivizes honesty. I don't grade a lot of student classwork in chemistry or physics. In fact, I will often tell them something like this up front: "You have thirty minutes to get this done, then we'll go over the answers. This is a completion grade, because it's just for you to practice. Yes, you could obviously cheat on it. And your cheating would become very obvious on next week's test, when you have no clue how to do any of this because you copied answers today." In fact, a lot of times, I will hand out the answers with the worksheet, or go ahead and put them on the board.

I don't need the student to be honest with me about what they know. I've been teaching for twenty years, and I'm good at my job. *I already know what they know.* I need the student to learn to be honest with *themselves* about what they know. The point of the assignment is for the student to realize, "Oh crap. I don't know how to balance net ionic equations. I better get some help before the test gets here."

Parker Palmer, author of *The Courage to Teach*, puts it this way: "To teach is to create a space where obedience to the truth is practiced."

And always remember: Students are incentivized by American educational culture (and their parents) to care about grades more than they care about learning. So the less you grade, the more you force the student to deal with learning as the primary objective in the room.

Second, I take the job seriously enough to avoid the shortcuts that come with the curriculum whenever possible.

As I write this, it's 2019. If you're using a pre-packaged curriculum, it is 100 percent certain that the solutions are already widely available online[1] and your students will lean on those solutions if you let them. Students respect teachers who respect the class enough to write their own material, or at least edit the pre-packaged material so that "teaching" means something more than "Turn to the next page in the manual and hand out worksheet 47-C."

There are all sorts of creative, uncheatable ways to do this. One option: Give them a multiple-choice quiz, but all the correct answers are already bubbled in. The quiz instructions are: "Explain why each correct answer is correct." This works well because questions that require effective communication are always more meaningful—and harder to cheat—than questions that merely require transmission of data. Is a quiz like that harder to grade? You bet. But if your class can be scored by a Scantron machine, you're essentially unnecessary in the Google/Khan Academy/Edgenuity era.

Third—and most importantly—I only discipline actual behavior, not potential behavior.

I have no problem with creating multiple versions of the test, providing cover sheets, or isolating test-takers—as long as those decisions are rooted in actual observed behavior, rather than the assumption of inevitable misbehavior.

I once had a student hand me a dentist's note as an excuse for missing a test. I knew when he handed it to me that it was fraudulent, because I'd heard him earlier in the hallway, telling a classmate about going to watch his older sister at a collegiate event the day before. I

---

1 Slader.com, anyone?

smiled, thanked him, and went to call and verify the dentist's excuse. That call turned into an adventure, because the dentist's office had a lot of questions about how he had acquired the excuse, and people in medical fields are a bit picky about things like having their names used on faked documents.

Armed with an assurance from the dentist that the student had not, in fact, been in their office the previous day, I called his mother to ask about the excuse. She was furious that I didn't trust her son, until I told her that the only reason I had called was because I over-heard her son talking about what he'd actually been doing the day before. Can you imagine how much more difficult that call would have been if I'd only been able to say, "Well, I just don't trust your son by default"?

Operating this way has one unfortunate side effect: some people are definitely going to get away with some things. But here's the thing: How many of us would vote for a politician who ran on a promise of legislation that would require a device on all vehicles to prevent them from breaking the posted speed limit? I wouldn't. But that's what we're doing as teachers when our default assumption is that all students are going to cheat all of the time on everything.

Certainly, there are times when class-wide (or campus-wide) discipline is called for. But those moments are few and far between, in my opinion. A former colleague uses a (very politically incorrect) metaphor to describe this behavior: he calls it "shotgun discipline." He uses it to refer to things like this:

- One student brings vodka to school in a water bottle. In response, the school declares that all water must be purchased at school.
- One student misuses a cell phone at break. In response, the school bans all cell phones from campus.[2]

---

2 It is 2019 and I just learned that a school within ten minutes of my house just re-enacted a campus-wide ban on phones. I wish them the best of luck in that battle; they're going to need it.

- One student gets caught smoking in the bathroom. In response, the school forces all students to take scheduled, monitored bathroom breaks.[3]

Unfortunately, some people are still going to lie, no matter what. They've made that decision, and you can't talk them out of it. Those are not the people whose hearts and minds you're likely to capture as a teacher, sad as it is to say. Being human means the choice to be less than human is always available, after all. But going overboard to ensure cheaters never get away with anything may have the unfortunate side effect of also ensuring that students who are struggling toward decency never actually trust you enough to learn from you.

Again, all of this gets easier when you think about it from your own perspective. How do you feel in faculty meetings when the staff is being chewed out over something, and everyone in the room knows that only two teachers actually made the mistake being discussed? That's exactly how the classroom feels when teachers throw around shotgun-discipline policies rather than dealing with students as individual human beings.

And I can attest from experience: approaching hard cases with trust and open hands does something to many of them. For some students who are accustomed to being treated with well-deserved suspicion, a single teacher refusing to buy into the narrative that they're broken beyond repair can work wonders. (Not all, of course, as we discussed on the previous page.)

It won't happen instantly, of course. There are actually precious few moments in education that look like *Dead Poets Society* or

---

3 I have a former colleague currently working in a school at which every class is lined up, counted off, and marched to the bathroom by their teacher. This includes seniors who are less than twelve months away from being turned loose with near-absolute freedom on college campuses, hundreds of miles from their parents. I shudder to think about how ill prepared such students are going to be to handle that freedom.

Dangerous Minds. But over time, trust can have a restorative effect. That's why I love that Parker Palmer quote about obedience to the truth being "practiced." The notion of practice carries with it the assumption that this will take work, time, and repetition.

One of my favorite authors is Kentucky tobacco farmer Wendell Berry. His poem "Manifesto: The Mad Farmer Liberation Front" contains some of my favorite lines. In fact, a portion is framed on my porch wall as I type: "Laughter is immeasurable. Be joyful though you have considered all the facts . . . Practice resurrection."

Trust is a practice. You won't get it right a lot of the time, and neither will they. But, over time, we are all practicing our way toward the human beings we eventually hope to be.

Humans cheat. They always have, and they always will. Trust on.

WE ARE ALL PRACTICING OUR WAY TOWARD THE HUMAN BEINGS WE EVENTUALLY HOPE TO BE.

HUMAN HOMEWORK

1. Spend a class period asking about the motivations behind cheating. Let them see that the "why" matters more than the "what" or the "how." In other words, students cheat for two reasons: either they lack integrity of character, or they got into a jam and panicked. In either case, the underlying issue is much more important than the momentary grade. This is well worth taking the time to discuss and make explicit.

2. Consider your grading and assessment structure: Are you inadvertently incentivizing cheating in some way by how you've set up your coursework? (You might want to revisit the discussion about homework and grading from chapter four.)

3. A lot of cheating happens because of deadlines. Therefore, the fewer hard deadlines you have, the less cheating you'll deal with. Even when a hard deadline is involved, I'm clear with my students that coming to me with a reasonable request for an extension is likely to result in a small deduction, whereas cheating is guaranteed to result in no credit. Based on these ideas, work with your students to create a deadline/cheating policy that the entire class is on board with.

4. Tell your students up front: "I choose to trust you until you give me a reason not to." Then have them discuss what behaviors might give you a reason to withdraw some of that trust.

ELEVEN

HUMANS BUILD

I once watched a group of boys on our playground. For the entire time they were allotted at recess (which was, thankfully, unstructured time), they moved bark with cups. We had recently gotten a fresh load of bark delivered to spruce up the space, so it was very loosely packed, and they were using their cups to pick it up, one cup at a time, carrying it about fifteen feet, and dropping it in a new spot. After about twenty minutes, they had created a pretty sizable hill.

Mesmerized by their task, I finally wandered over from the sidewalk to chat.

"Hey, guys. Whatcha doing?"

"Building," one of them told me.

"Yes, but what are you building?"

He gave me the look that elementary students have given clueless adults since the beginning of time. "A hill."

Ah, yes. A hill. How had I failed to see it?

"Okay. Cool. But what for?"

He regarded me as if I needed my very own "dealing with children" IEP before calmly responding: "To stand on." Thoroughly schooled in the unassailable logic of childhood, I walked away with a smile on my face.

It's innate: We build things. From our earliest days stacking measuring cups in the kitchen floor, to the obsession we get in our fifties with padding our 401(k)s before retirement, we are built to build. And, left to our own devices, we're happiest when we're building—so long as the thing we're building is freely chosen.

Building is good. It's necessary. Done properly, it brings great meaning to our lives—and the lives of our students. However, "building" isn't what most of our students spend time doing. For many of our students, there's no mental connection between the way they spend their time in school and the life they hope to eventually build for themselves—especially in that time between sixth grade and eleventh grade, which I have come to refer to as "the abyss," because it's where many seemingly bright, motivated students simply . . . vanish. After a couple of years in the abyss, they're replaced with people who don't want to learn and definitely hate this class and don't understand why they're even here, and will they ever even need to know this stuff after high school?

WE'RE HAPPIEST WHEN WE'RE BUILDING—SO LONG AS THE THING WE'RE BUILDING IS FREELY CHOSEN.

I originally titled this section "Humans Work," but that wasn't quite right, because "work" has a negative connotation in our culture. Many people work all week so we can spend the weekends building memories with our families. We work from twenty-five to sixty so we can spend our retirement building relationships with our grandchildren. Lots of us do all we can to avoid work, and we celebrate when we get an unexpected day off.

It's our job as human teachers to reclaim the abyss and help students connect the things we're asking them to do to the lives we're helping them build. One reason students loathe school so much is because the "work" they do in school doesn't in any way resemble the work they see performed by the adults they respect. It's routine, repetitive, and devoid of meaning.

Think of the part of your job you hate the most. The part that doesn't really connect in any way to why you chose the job in the first place. The irrational, meaningless, paint-by-numbers part that any robot or sufficiently trained domestic animal could do. Then imagine it fifty minutes at a time, six or seven times a day. That is the lived experience of millions of students.

This is bigger than simply writing better lesson plans or changing the curriculum you use in your classroom. One of my favorite basketball coaches runs a summer camp in Tennessee every year.[1] In meetings with coaches, while players are in drill work, he repeats the same phrase about ten thousand times a summer: "Culture eats strategy for breakfast."

The phrase originated with the late Peter Drucker, a management consultant and *Wall Street Journal* columnist—but Coach T has made it his raison d'être. He pounds this idea into the head of every coach he comes across, young or old: it doesn't matter what you're doing if the kids don't understand why you're doing it.

Coach T knows *X*s and *O*s, certainly, and he can run a whiteboard as well as any other coach I've ever been around. But where he distinguishes himself—where you can distinguish yourself and set yourself apart from every other teacher in your students' lives—is in his relentless pursuit of team culture. It's evident in the past players who come back to work his camps, and in the current players who

---

1 Hey, Kevin Templeton!

officiate, and in the coaches who have been attending his camps and listening to him for years. The man has made a career out of building culture.

In my classroom, there are a few key words I try to build culture around every year:

INTELLECT

I make it very obvious up front that intellectual performance is at a premium in my classroom, because cognitive abilities and accomplishments definitely impact the lives they'll get to lead after high school. If I'm teaching middle school students in the abyss, I work a "Nerds Run the World" lecture into the first week every year. I tell them things like "If you can learn geometry without doing a single homework assignment, more power to you. We don't make the kids that can dunk wear ankle weights on the basketball court." But I make it obvious to them that when I say things like "intellectual performance," I mean the finished product of their efforts, not the innate ability they bring to the class out of the gate.

RESPECT

I thank the students for coming at the beginning of each class (or I try to), and I make it obvious to them that I will respect them as human beings, regardless of their academic performance. I handle discipline from a framework of mutual respect, and (as much as possible) I never waste their time intentionally with cheesy, just-because work.

CURIOSITY

I tell them that they should always feel free to interrupt to ask questions about anything we talk about, or anything else that occurs to them. I tell them that if I don't know, I'll say so and look for the answer. I tell them if I can't carve out time for their question immediately, I'll do it as soon as I can. (And I give them permission to assign a To-Do to me in Basecamp to make sure I remember. It always blows them away when I send them an email later telling them I spent an hour researching their question). We once spent most of a physics class researching the history of the trebuchet when a kid asked me how to pronounce it. It was a fantastic day.

READING

I don't talk about reading as a "You should feel guilty if you don't like to read" sort of thing. Instead, we talk about the way reading leads to autonomy. Students crave power over their lives more than almost anything else, so I leverage that natural human instinct to drive home the message "If you learn to read and research, the whole wide world is open to you for the rest of your life." But I also make sure they understand: "Every college professor is going to assume you read 250 words per minute, and it's impossible to get better at something you never do." Frequently, if I miss a math or science class, I'll assign articles from Longreads rather than the sort of worksheets or cookie-cutter assignments they're used to when they have subs in other courses.

I build my classroom culture around these four things because I'm intentionally telling the students, "These four things are tools you can use to build whatever life you're trying to build." Smart, curious, respectful people who love to solve problems on their own are the most valuable employees in every organization on the planet, from my local car wash to the UN.

And something amazing happens when students begin to see you as a co-builder in their life, rather than a gatekeeper who keeps them from doing what they want. They start building. They start to take ownership of their role in the classroom, because they see it as a piece of the rest of their life, rather than the thing *keeping them from the rest of their life.*

For the past several years, I've taught junior and senior literature and composition in a combined classroom. These are the students that don't take dual enrollment or AP courses. And every January, I tell them: "On May nineteenth, you're going to stand in the gym while strangers walk around, and you're going to talk to anyone who wants to listen about your eight-page research paper. Total strangers will grade your research and communication, and the biggest grade of the fourth quarter will come from that evaluation. So by Monday, I need you to have an idea about what interests you enough that you could spend four months researching it."

They are always initially terrified. Then the questions begin: "What do we write about?"

"I don't know," I tell them. "What are you interested in? What do you want to the spend the rest of your life knowing about?" This year, I got papers on schizophrenia, serial killers, reproductive rights, the impact of music on memory, how to distinguish a religion from a cult, gender disparities in Hollywood salaries, psychopathy, the college athletic recruiting process, and more. In the past, I've been blown away by papers about offshoring manufacturing jobs, Calvinism, and the effect of lowered infrastructure funding on Alabama's bridges. (I still shiver and think about that one every time I drive over a bridge, Sterling.)

And every May, the parents and teachers who leave the room give glowing reviews. In fact, they frequently give the students much higher marks than I do. Because a seventeen-year-old student talking animatedly about a topic they're deeply invested in is so far outside the norm of what most adults expect of high school students, they genuinely don't have a frame of reference for anything like that.

But I do, because unlike them, I've been in the room with the kids for four months. Watching them build.

HUMAN HOMEWORK

1. Come up with four or five "touchstones" you'd like to build your classroom culture on. Use them to brand your room, just like if you were a PR executive at a restaurant chain. The more you involve your students in this exercise, the more they'll internalize what you're doing.

2. Dedicate a class or two each semester to simply talking with students about what they're building: short-term (this year), mid-term (college), and long-term (adult life). Help them connect what they do in your classroom to their own goals. But remember that it's highly likely that their goals won't be academic, and that's okay. In fact, it's more helpful if they're not, because it opens up a way for you to connect their school life to their life after high school: Oh, you want to make graphic novels? Don't you think that would be easier with an art degree? Now let's talk about what ACT score would get you a scholarship to a school with a good art program.

3. No matter what class you teach, do the semester-long self-guided paper assignment. Trust me. It's the one thing all year they'll be proudest of.

CONCLUSION

So here we are. The end. This book is more manifesto than how-to. I think that's a good thing, and I hope you agree. The fundamental problem of education isn't one of technology, or curriculum, or funding. The fundamental problem is philosophical, relational.

One of the things I worry about in writing a book like this is something Dave Burgess said to me in my initial pitch to him about it. He told me, "You're saying good things. But a lot of people who will be drawn to your book will already believe those things, and a lot of people who disagree will never read the book anyway."

I think he's right about that, to a degree. People drawn to a book called *Student Equals Human* probably *already* view their students as human beings. And people who took one look at the cover, sneered at the title, and turned away probably are never going to. Still, there's one giant reason I thought it was worth the time and effort it took to get these words down in print.

Student equals human, yes. But so does teacher. And humans need company.

Even if you agreed with everything I said in this book before you read it, there's immense value in realizing you're not alone. For those of you who look around, frustrated at the fact that our educational system seems to be failing so many students you're trying your hardest to help, it's important to realize that there are far more of us on the same page than we realize, simply because it can be difficult to put your ideas out there in an educational culture that often seems designed to strip people of their humanity and treat them like interchangeable parts.

It's easy to sit at the lunch table and gripe about the students, recycling the same old tropes adults have used to minimize the children in their charge since industrialized schools began. It's easy to assume that they'll begin being human once they get their diploma or make it to college. It's easy to flow in the current you find yourself floating in, even if you grasp that it's headed nowhere good.

But maybe just walking around with the book, or talking about it with colleagues, can open up conversations about some of the faulty assumptions at the root of our classrooms. If this book provides a common phrase that teachers like us can rally around—"Student Equals Human"—perhaps that simple idea can connect teachers to a movement that can change the lived experience of thousands or millions of students.

So fight the grumps. They're losing anyway. Let them sneer on, until they look around one day and (hopefully) realize they've become a tiny minority in our profession. Because this is our profession. And the faster the grumps become uncomfortable enough to change (or leave), the better off our students will be. And you, dear reader, are not a grump.

Yes, fight the grumps—but don't hate the grumps. I can't; I was once one of them. I came into education with an authoritarian view of students that was the byproduct—whether accidental or intentional—of the way I was raised, the churches and schools I attended as a child, and the attitudes of many of the adults that influenced me in my youth. I'm walking proof that how we view students can be overhauled, freely and of our own volition, if we're simply willing to say this every day: I'm human. They're human. How would I like to be treated if I were in my own classroom?

This simple classroom idea connects to a much larger (and much more important) point. We live in a culture that is facing a crisis of civility. Our political process seems more dysfunctional by the day, our lives online are constantly subject to toxicity beyond belief, and our daily lives are subject to explosions of rage that seem incomprehensible.

A few years ago, I described a professional disagreement this way to a friend: "We can't agree on the most basic of terms. It's as if we're looking at a painting. I say, 'That's a pretty good fire truck,' and he responds with, 'Fire truck? This is a painting of a watermelon!' We don't see different aspects of the same thing; somehow, we look at the same situation and see two completely different objects."

I think about that metaphor a lot when I watch the news or scroll social media these days. We seem culturally hell-bent on dividing ourselves into continuous, ever-smaller slices of identity. Even our conservative and liberal group identities have fractured into ever-smaller niches at war for ideological supremacy. What we are witnessing is the logical outcome of a society that constantly tempts us to treat human beings inhumanely.

But how do we stem the tide? I'm never going to be president, and I'd last about five minutes in elected office before I began throwing chairs through plate glass windows out of sheer frustration at the mind-numbing bureaucracy of it all.

Instead, I've chosen to use my classroom as an opportunity to strike back—to insist that everyone in the room is a human being, and to declare in words and deeds that this shared identity matters far more than any other adjectives or labels we stack on top of it.

This book is an attempt to create more classrooms like that. There are students in all sorts of schools—public, charter, private, parochial—but K–12 education remains the single most widely shared experience for most people. So the classroom seems to hold the most promise for changing the way a generation thinks—about themselves, their neighbors, and the grace and liberty they owe one another.

Be human. Love humans. School and life don't have to be much more complicated than that.

ACKNOWLEDGMENTS

Dave, thanks for taking a pitch from a complete Twitter rando.

Sal and team, thanks for getting a blob of ideas into this much more palatable rectangular form.

I've been blessed to work with fantastic people for years, many of whom have put up with all manner of half-formed ideas that would eventually become this book. Thanks for your patience, all.

James Johnson provided back porch chats that were quite useful in sorting out a lot of this, and he also once talked me out of branding myself.

I owe a debt of gratitude to every student who's ever come through my classroom. Each of you has taught me something that matters, and collectively you have all made me much better at being human. To their parents: thank you for trusting me with your children.

Laura, Macybug, JackMan, and Ellie Belly make my house the sort of place where we can talk loud about big ideas and giggle hard about little joys. Y'all are the reason any of my life makes any sense at all to me.

Also coffee: it is the very best thing.

ABOUT THE AUTHOR

JAY ADAMS is currently head of school at Edgewood Academy in Elmore, Alabama. A graduate of Lee University, he holds teaching certificates in English, math, and science. Over the past twenty years, he has taught courses in literature, physics, chemistry, math, theology, logic, documentary film, leadership, and more.

He should write more often about education at studentequalshuman.com, but he has a bad habit of procrastinating by strumming the guitar on his back porch instead. Adams lives in the Montgomery area with his wife Laura; their children Macy, Jack Tyler, and Ellie Kate; and Eliza Jane the Very Dumbest Dog.

MORE FROM

DAVE BURGESS Consulting, Inc.

Since 2012, DBCI has been publishing books that inspire and equip educators to be their best. For more information on our titles or to purchase bulk orders for your school, district, or book study, visit DaveBurgessConsulting.com/DBCIbooks.

MORE INSPIRATION, PROFESSIONAL GROWTH & PERSONAL DEVELOPMENT

Be REAL by Tara Martin

Be the One for Kids by Ryan Sheehy

The Coach ADVenture by Amy Illingworth

Creatively Productive by Lisa Johnson

Educational Eye Exam by Alicia Ray

The EduNinja Mindset by Jennifer Burdis

Empower Our Girls by Lynmara Colón and Adam Welcome

Finding Lifelines by Andrew Grieve and Andrew Sharos

The Four O'Clock Faculty by Rich Czyz

How Much Water Do We Have? by Pete and Kris Nunweiler

P Is for Pirate by Dave and Shelley Burgess

A Passion for Kindness by Tamara Letter

The Path to Serendipity by Allyson Apsey

Sanctuaries by Dan Tricarico

The SECRET SAUCE by Rich Czyz

Shattering the Perfect Teacher Myth by Aaron Hogan

Stories from Webb by Todd Nesloney

Talk to Me by Kim Bearden

Teach Better by Chad Ostrowski, Tiffany Ott, Rae Hughart, and Jeff Gargas

Teach Me, Teacher by Jacob Chastain

Teach, Play, Learn! by Adam Peterson

TeamMakers by Laura Robb and Evan Robb

Through the Lens of Serendipity by Allyson Apsey

The Zen Teacher by Dan Tricarico

LIKE A PIRATE™ SERIES

Teach Like a PIRATE by Dave Burgess

eXPlore Like a Pirate by Michael Matera

Learn Like a Pirate by Paul Solarz

Play Like a Pirate by Quinn Rollins

Run Like a Pirate by Adam Welcome

Tech Like a PIRATE by Matt Miller

LEAD LIKE A PIRATE™ SERIES

Lead Like a PIRATE by Shelley Burgess and Beth Houf

Balance Like a Pirate by Jessica Cabeen, Jessica Johnson, and Sarah Johnson

Lead beyond Your Title by Nili Bartley

Lead with Appreciation by Amber Teamann and Melinda Miller

Lead with Culture by Jay Billy

Lead with Instructional Rounds by Vicki Wilson

Lead with Literacy by Mandy Ellis

LEADERSHIP & SCHOOL CULTURE

Fight Song by Kim Bearden

Culturize by Jimmy Casas

Escaping the School Leader's Dunk Tank by Rebecca Coda and Rick Jetter

From Teacher to Leader by Starr Sackstein

The Innovator's Mindset by George Couros

It's OK to Say "They" by Christy Whittlesey

Kids Deserve It! by Todd Nesloney and Adam Welcome

Live Your Excellence by Jimmy Casas

Let Them Speak by Rebecca Coda and Rick Jetter

The Limitless School by Abe Hege and Adam Dovico

Next-Level Teaching by Jonathan Alsheimer

The Pepper Effect by Sean Gaillard

The Principled Principal by Jeffrey Zoul and Anthony McConnell

Relentless by Hamish Brewer

The Secret Solution by Todd Whitaker, Sam Miller, and Ryan Donlan

Start. Right. Now. by Todd Whitaker, Jeffrey Zoul, and Jimmy Casas

Stop. Right. Now. by Jimmy Casas and Jeffrey Zoul

Teach Your Class Off by CJ Reynolds

They Call Me "Mr. De" by Frank DeAngelis

Unmapped Potential by Julie Hasson and Missy Lennard

When Kids Lead by Todd Nesloney and Adam Dovico

Word Shift by Joy Kirr

Your School Rocks by Ryan McLane and Eric Lowe

TECHNOLOGY & TOOLS

50 Things You Can Do with Google Classroom by Alice Keeler and Libbi Miller

50 Things to Go Further with Google Classroom by Alice Keeler and Libbi Miller

140 Twitter Tips for Educators by Brad Currie, Billy Krakower, and Scott Rocco

Block Breaker by Brian Aspinall

Code Breaker by Brian Aspinall

Control Alt Achieve by Eric Curts

Google Apps for Littles by Christine Pinto and Alice Keeler

Master the Media by Julie Smith

Reality Bytes by Christine Lion-Bailey, Jesse Lubinsky, Micah Shippee, PhD

Sail the 7 Cs with Microsoft Education by Becky Keene and Kathi Kersznowski

Shake Up Learning by Kasey Bell

Social LEADia by Jennifer Casa-Todd

Stepping up to Google Classroom by Alice Keeler and Kimberly Mattina

Teaching Math with Google Apps by Alice Keeler and Diana Herrington

Teachingland by Amanda Fox and Mary Ellen Weeks

TEACHING METHODS & MATERIALS

All 4s and 5s by Andrew Sharos

Boredom Busters by Katie Powell

The Classroom Chef by John Stevens and Matt Vaudrey

The Collaborative Classroom by Trevor Muir

Copyrighteous by Diana Gill

Ditch That Homework by Matt Miller and Alice Keeler

Ditch That Textbook by Matt Miller

Don't Ditch That Tech by Matt Miller, Nate Ridgway, and
Angelia Ridgway

EDrenaline Rush by John Meehan

Educated by Design by Michael Cohen, The Tech Rabbi

The EduProtocol Field Guide by Marlena Hebern and
Jon Corippo

The EduProtocol Field Guide: Book 2 by Marlena Hebern and
Jon Corippo

Instant Relevance by Denis Sheeran

LAUNCH by John Spencer and A.J. Juliani

Make Learning MAGICAL by Tisha Richmond

Pure Genius by Don Wettrick

The Revolution by Darren Ellwein and Derek McCoy

Shift This! by Joy Kirr

Skyrocket Your Teacher Coaching by Michael Cary Sonbert

Spark Learning by Ramsey Musallam

Sparks in the Dark by Travis Crowder and Todd Nesloney

Table Talk Math by John Stevens

The Wild Card by Hope and Wade King

The Writing on the Classroom Wall by Steve Wyborney

CHILDREN'S BOOKS

Beyond Us by Aaron Polansky

Cannonball In by Tara Martin

Dolphins in Trees by Aaron Polansky

I Want to Be a Lot by Ashley Savage

The Princes of Serendip by Allyson Apsey

The Wild Card Kids by Hope and Wade King

Zom-Be a Design Thinker by Amanda Fox